POEMS

Alan Ross

POEMS

Selected and with an Introduction by
David Hughes

THE HARVILL PRESS
LONDON

The poems in this volume are chosen from the following works by Alan Ross: *The Derelict Day* (John Lehmann, 1947), *Something of the Sea* (Derek Verschoyle, 1954), *To Whom It May Concern* (Hamish Hamilton, 1958), *African Negatives* (Eyre & Spottiswoode, 1967), *The Taj Express* (London Magazine Editions, 1973), *Open Sea* (London Magazine Editions, 1975), *Death Valley and Other Poems in America* (London Magazine Editions, 1980), *Blindfold Games* (Harvill, 1986), *Coastwise Lights* (Harvill, 1988), *After Pusan* (Harvill, 1995), *Winter Sea* (Harvill, 1997)

Published by The Harvill Press, 2005

2 4 6 8 9 7 5 3 1

First published in Great Britain in 2005 by
The Harvill Press
Random House, 20 Vauxhall Bridge Road,
London SWIV 2SA

Random House Australia (Pty) Limited
20 Alfred Street, Milsons Point, Sydney,
New South Wales 2061, Australia

Random House New Zealand Limited
18 Poland Road, Glenfield,
Auckland 10, New Zealand

Random House (Pty) Limited
Endulini, 5A Jubilee Road, Parktown 2193, South Africa

The Random House Group Limited Reg. No. 954009
www.randomhouse.co.uk

A CIP catalogue record for this book
is available from the British Library

ISBN 1 84343 224 2

Papers used by Random House are natural,
recyclable products made from wood grown in sustainable forests;
the manufacturing processes conform to the environmental
regulations of the country of origin

Typeset in Baskerville by Palimpsest Book Production Limited
Printed and bound in Great Britain by Clays Ltd, St Ives plc

Introduction

A STATEMENT OF affection as well as esteem, this page or
two is less a preface than a prelude: not intended as criti-
cism at a serious level or biography at a more basic one,
just a personal introduction to a friend, as at a party, want-
ing to share his company with others, though for his sake
and mine trying to keep things informal; then getting
myself out of the way.

I knew Alan Ross for next to half a century. We met not
that often but at intervals, which is no contradiction in a
friendship which always took up where it left off, and usually
on his home ground in London and Sussex which never
changed. Without his seeing any need to compromise, his
habits of life lasted a lifetime, and his poetry celebrates
that commitment to one or two special places, balanced by
an appetite for travel that took him all over the world. A
year before his death in 2001, he asked me to help him put
together an edition of his collected poems. Here they are,
not "collected" in the academic sense that not a line is left
out, but a full choice, no doubt with omissions Alan would
regret and entries he might shudder to see revived.

In the first of a series of volumes of elegant self-
exploration composed in his two last decades, Alan wrote
in *Blindfold Games* (1985) that its chapters of prose inter-
woven with verse, embodying his life to the age of twenty-
four, were "only incidentally an autobiography; more
accurately they represent the material out of which I began
to write poetry".

Never an egotist, always in tones of restraint, he tracks

his course from birth in 1922 in a Calcutta household of moderate privilege within sight and sound of cricket, but visited by such childhood terrors as a snake falling into his bath, through the slightly lesser horrors of exile – he was only seven when sent to England – at a prep-school in Sussex, and on to Haileybury where despite an almost foppish languor he was a top player in most games, not least squash and cricket. For four terms he marked time at Oxford before call-up in 1941, spent three years of perilous service in the Royal Navy as a rating in escort destroyers on Arctic convoys to Russia, was then commissioned and posted to ships defending the East coast of England, before being moved on to Germany as an intelligence officer based in Hamburg. That was already quite a life to have lived, one frequently close to death. At worst he was trapped for hours behind a bulkhead on a sinking destroyer amid the drowned corpses of men he knew. With better luck, when he was prowling Soho one night on leave, his room at the Regent Palace Hotel was destroyed by a bomb.

All this, with exile ("the idea of India growing in me as I grew up") and home ("during my sea-time I used to dream of Sussex as a generalised, romantic image conjured out of memory and hope") simmering beneath the surface, helped to turn him into a poet of warm feeling who was also a cool reporter. "When eventually I came to write what I wanted about those years I stuck to what was real – life on board a destroyer in wartime, as I experienced it. No more, no less." If suitably softer, even his love poems are just as real and tough, still with the grit of despatches from the front line.

The first poems, including the convoy mini-epic entitled "J.W.51B", appear to date in origin from 1942. Though that poem came out in 1947, Ross wrote, "In the rush of leaving Harwich for the Admiralty my poem notebook got lost.

It surfaced later, but it took nearly twenty years, and a return to wartime places, for me to be able to put the poems of that time together again." In such asides of Alan's there is something casual, as though it did not do to make a big thing of his poetry. But the effect of his poems of war at sea bit gradually deeper as peace took over, increasing in resonance, as did those of fellows whose work he admired in other theatres of war, Keith Douglas and Alun Lewis. His post-war poem "The Sea 1939–1945", a group of half a dozen sonnets dropped by Alan from his later collections, is celebrated in Adam Piette's *Imagination at War* (1995), a study which reaches its peroration by hailing Ross as "one of the very best poets of the war". I round off this selection with those sonnets, thus returning in the end to a young man who was to occupy much of his inner life with exploring, in sport, sex, art, the tensions of war and peace. Otherwise the poems are presented in more or less the order in which they were written. They make a good story.

When the muse stirred, Alan preferred backs of envelopes to sheets of paper. Yet his verse, though he was shy by nature and oblique by temperament, was the one place where he never concealed between the lines his essential privacy; in the prose memoirs his life's loves earn barely a mention. (Names slip only privily into the poems; in "Winter Boats at Brighton" there are "bows bearing loved names" beached on the shingle, one of them Deirdre, the future Mrs Cyril Connolly.) Against all appearance this idle dandy, that particular languor he sported tinged with a cafard that led to a number of disorders of mind from the early '60s onwards, was a good working journalist, both as a sports reporter on the *Observer* from 1950 to 1971 and as a strikingly original editor of *London Magazine* for forty years, and he applied the trade rules of both functions – urgency, immediacy, coherence, bringing tomorrow up to date by looking hard at yesterday – to the art that not only mattered most to him but received the best of his effortless gift of never seeming to do a stroke of work: poetry (in 1961 he took over editorship of the *London Magazine* from John Lehmann, who first published Alan's poems in *Penguin New Writing*).

Despite having a father of impeccably British origin in India, a coal-mining businessman appointed (like his son) CBE, and his mother Clare Fitzpatrick, daughter of an Indian Army officer, but with Armenian antecedents, somehow Alan's features were a fond caricature of an Indian statesman at his most enigmatic; his seven years of boyhood on the subcontinent looked as though they had rubbed off on him. His appearance was quietly magnificent, made for a guru: a domed head with a sleek sweep of black hair that hardly greyed, a strong nose, lips on which sensuality and sensitivity fought out their own game with humour, eyes for the most part calmly amused, yet now and then bulging with indignation or puzzlement. He had an athletic walk, a relaxed mien: his body was always as strong a presence as his mind, both as flexible as those of a natural athlete and a wit until far into his seventies. Raffishly dressed in his own smart style, tweed jacket and coloured cords, scarlet-lined overcoat, flash of a scarf above a favourite shirt fraying at the collar, he always fitted in while looking quite unlike anyone else.

For a man who travelled the world, reporting on cricket tours in Australia, South Africa, the West Indies, not to mention ample holidays in southern Europe that gave rise to such books as *Time Was Away* (on Corsica in 1948), in which he secretively distanced himself from the action by never using the word "I", and *The Bandit on the Billiard Table* (on Sardinia in 1954), real home for Alan was limited to a locality: he was wedded to London SW3 and SW7, the upper bohemia where Chelsea's denim brushes Kensington's pinstripe, strolling over the years between the magazine's one-man office in Thurloe Place and a variety of homes in the vicinity where the entertaining ranged from the grand apogee of a dinner in Pelham Crescent and, as his publisher once put it, "the peculiar splendour of a kitchen supper *chez* Ross".

As a youth Alan had settled post-war in an Elm Park Gardens flat; half a century later he died only yards away at his cottage in Elm Park Lane. After marrying Jennifer Fry in 1949 he became singularly devoted to Clayton, their manor house north of Brighton ("downland country, a smell of the sea") in his beloved Sussex, close to the cricket land-scape of his youth, happiest source of verse that set out without any plan but with purpose to order future, past, present, to his own satisfaction. Here in Clayton, in the heart of his life, he reconciled his life's themes. First, he hung the paintings he had bought in youth – Pasmore, Nolan, Drysdale, Vaughan – later selling them when he or the magazine was short of cash. His own painterly skills show in the always graphic similes in the verse.

Next, his passion for sport was paramount; he was a racing man, betting daily, owning horses, often winning. Of earlier days he wrote that "the shiver down the spine" produced by a Housman stanza (he had MacNeice in his pocket when he joined up) or a passage of music was never matched by the grace of a bowler's action or a sweetly executed late cut: "first steps in the evolution of a sensi-bility slow to come to terms with itself", he added, but the delight persisted: his poems on a stroke by Gower, the action of a racehorse, a mesmeric dribble by Stanley Matthews, are still "as good a way as I could imagine of relating techniques to aesthetics".

Between the '50s and the '70s I spent weekends in luxury's

lap at Clayton, such stars of his second volume of memoirs, *Coastwise Lights* (1988), as William Plomer, Cyril Connolly, T.C.Worsley often present for a Sunday roast, with good doses of the racecourse at Plumpton and the Hove cricket ground for further diversion. Between overs or races we shared oblique news of our affairs. A patina of gossip enabled us to skate over more private concerns, unless they truly mattered. When two or three times mental crisis threatened his life, we met more often, as did other close friends, he in pain at breakdown, we in despair at inability to help. For long spells Alan was suicidal, twice trying to cut his wrists, but he had a writer's suspicion of psychotherapy, a fear of its killing more than it might cure.

Every reader of these poems, indeed this long tale of a poem which packs the not just melancholy nor quite comic punch of a narrative, might well see in it a twentieth-century testament that captured our faults, hesitations, doubts. In the mix of imagery between women and war and games, the conflation of nature in the world and art on the wall, here is a lifetime distilled in short inter-relating lyrics that strike echoes into one another. I find in them too a nudge of my own memories, or travels, caught on the hop. In *Selected Poems* by Lawrence Durrell, which Alan edited in 1977, he wrote of his subject, "No-one has written more mnemonically about landscape" – an adverbial choice apt for Alan's own poems abroad.

In two further works, half memoirs, half travel, in the last decade of his life Alan Ross, with his future wife Jane Rye, went on the roam again, often to such old haunts as the islands off the west of Italy and the north of Sicily visited in youth, or to the sites of old wounds in the Arctic re-opened to see if they had healed, now and then exploring a territory unknown. But they are mostly about unlocking memories, setting a perspective which he felt his life

x

needed as it neared an end. In *After Pusan* (1995) he flew east to South Korea and India flooded back to him and he glimpsed his childhood anew. In *Winter Sea* (1997) he returned to northern waters and the countries fringing his war experience, the Norwegian coast at Bergen, the Baltic at Tallinn, and back to Hamburg where for him hostilities had ended. In each case new poems, as tautly fluent as ever, poured forth in dying falls. Once again Ross is continuing to tell, sidelong, at a remove, deeply, the inward story of a life that looked outward into sport, society, fashion, art, girls, beaches, bars, travel, but mostly knew, and saw everything in terms of, that desperate war.

It was Christopher MacLehose, Alan's faithful publisher over many years, who commissioned this volume for Harvill and gave me (that liberating euphemism for the back of an envelope) *carte blanche*. Alan's friend the translator Euan Cameron, an editor with whom I lunch pleasurably in the established Ross style, eased me through the press with his gentle advice. I am grateful to Paul Zuckerman for helping so kindly. Alan's love of his middle years, Liz Claridge, who shares the American poems with him and much else, was exceptional in her support. In Italy I have forged with Margaret Vyner, whose life was bound up with Alan's in ways hidden deep inside the poems, what I hope is a friendship for good. I also hope that his step-daughter Victoria and his only son Jonathan, to both of whom Alan dedicated certain poems, will take pleasure in this edited self-portrait of the man they grew up with, a pride which I know their mother Jennifer, who died in 2003, would have shared.

But it is to Jane, companion of his last decade, fellow of his late travels, illustrator of his later books, wife for his last few months – of whose father Anthony Rye's poems Alan once wrote in a *Spectator* review of 1947 when Jane was four years old that "they are all beautifully observed, coherent and unsentimental", adjectives he might like applied now to his own prose and verse – yes, to Jane with much love I inscribe this volume, in the hope that she will think that it might gain Alan's not always easily earned approval. That rigour of his was why his *London Magazine* was so good a guide to his times, as are these poems to his life.

DAVID HUGHES

CONTENTS

PART I
At Sea

DESTROYERS IN THE ARCTIC

Camouflaged, they detach lengths of sea and sky
When they move; offset, speed and directions are a lie.

Everything is grey anyway; ships, water, snow, faces.
Flanking the convoy, we rarely go through our paces.

But sometimes on tightening waves at night they wheel
Drawing white moons on strings from dripping keel.

Cold cases them, like ships in glass; they are formal,
Not real, except in adversity. Such deception is normal.

At dusk they intensify dusk, strung out, non-committal:
Waves spill from our wake, crêpe paper magnetised by
    gun-metal.

They breathe silence, less solid than ghosts, ruminative
As the Arctic breaks up on their sides and they sieve

Moisture into mess-decks. Heat is cold-lined there,
Where we wait for a torpedo and lack air.

Repetitive of each other, imitating the sea's lift and fall,
On the wings of the convoy they indicate rehearsal.

Merchantmen move sideways, with the gait of crus-
    taceans,
Round whom like eels escorts take up their stations.

Landfall, Murmansk; but starboard now a lead-coloured
Island, Jan Mayen. Days identical, hoisted like sails,
    blurred.

3

Counters moved on an Admiralty map, snow like confetti
Covers the real us. We dream we are counterfeits tied to
  our jetty.

But cannot dream long; the sea curdles and sprawls,
Liverishly real, horizon and water tilting in to walls.

Staggering on deck and filthy
I watch the first stealthy
Feelers of light, the sky torn
And spurting, like blood from a thorn.

Nothing as fabulous as this
Has existed, the imperceptible kiss
Of sunlight on ice, on faces,
Withdrawn as it melts.

These black ships and welts
Of saffron streaking our mess,
Crate up and cradle all we possess,
Sunroses strewn over white horses.

The bulkhead sweating, and under naked bulbs
Men writing letters, playing ludo. The light
Cuts their arms off at the wrist, only the dice
Lives. Hammocks swing, nuzzling in tight
Like foals into flanks of mares. Bare shoulders
Glisten with oil, tattoo-marks rippling their scales on
Mermaids or girls' thighs as dice are shaken, cards
   played.
We reach for sleep like a gas, randy for oblivion.
But, laid out on lockers, some get waylaid;
And lie stiff, running off films in the mind's dark-room.
The air soupy, yet still cold; a beam sea rattles
Cups smelling of stale tea, knocks over a broom.
The light is watery, like the light of the sea-bed.
Marooned in it, stealthy as fishes, we may even be dead.

Standing on a ladder
Stretching for the top shelf, she'd swivel suddenly
And remark they were out of them,
Surprising the matelots craning their necks,
Her own rolled stocking-tops nipping plump thighs
Like the lips of balloons.

It was an old trick, often repeated,
But for a long time they fell for it,
Starved of stockings and silkiness,
And when she bid them come back
At the last moment before sailing,
They could never resist it,
Going to their graves with torpedoes of nylon.

MURMANSK

The snow whisper of bows through water
Asking and answer in their lift
And screw, ceremonials
Of salt and savagery,
Burial of man and mermaid.

On those last ski slopes
Voices still murmur
Ciels de Murmansk, ceilings, sea-eels,
Water-skiers with lovely backs
Arched before breaking.

I remember the thirst of Murmansk
The great eyelids of water.
Can one ever see through them?

NIGHT PATROL

We sail at dusk, the red moon
Like a paper lantern setting fire
To our wake. Headlands disappear,
Muffled in their own velvet.

Docks dwindle, rubbed out by mists,
Their cranes, like drunks, askew
Over jetties. Coal is unloaded
Under blue arc-lights.

Turning south, the mapped moon
Swings between masts, our aerials
Swollen and lurching. The bag
Of sea squirts black and sooty.

Flashes of gunfire, perhaps lightning,
Straddle our progress, a convoy
Of hearses. The bow-waves of gunboats
Sew us together, helplessly idling.

The watch changes, and changes
Again. We edge through a minefield,
Real or imaginary. The speed of a convoy
Is the speed of the slowest ship.

No one speaks, it might be a funeral.
Altering course, the moon congeals
On a new bearing. The telegraph rings,
And, at speed now, clouds grow visible.

We're on our own, making for harbour.
In tangerine light we sniff greenness,
Tremble like racehorses. Soon minesweepers
Pass us, continuing our business.

With the ship burning in their eyes
The white faces float like refuse
In the darkness – the water screwing
Oily circles where the hot steel lies.

They clutch with fingers frozen into claws
The lifebelts thrown from a destroyer,
And see, between the future's doors,
The gasping entrance of the sea.

Taken on board as many as lived, who
Had a mind left for living and the ocean,
They open eyes running with surf,
Heavy with the grey ghosts of explosion.

The meaning is not yet clear,
Where daybreak died in the smile –
And the mouth remained stiff
And grinning, stupid for a while.

But soon they joke, easy and warm,
As men will who have died once
Yet somehow were able to find their way –
Muttering this was not included in their pay.

Later, sleepless at night, the brain spinning
With cracked images, they won't forget
The confusion and the oily dead,
Nor yet the casual knack of living.

Waiting in the bar for the war to end,
Those who for the second time saw it begin
And, charting the future, watched death crawling
Like a lizard over the lidless eyes of the sun.
The shaving glass shows them now
The face and features that they find appalling.
Reflections of launches move across the mirror,
Destroyers and corvettes swinging round buoys, sweepers
At anchor. But here the voyages begin and end,
Gin-time stories which they note, like keepers
Of lightships, as they wait for news of friends –
The same routine, continuing the war until it ends.

The sea warmed glass, pink milk,
Such an evening of lull,
Of abandon. Men write letters
On deck, lean on the rails smoking.

Suddenly, out of nowhere, faint ripples
As if huge fish were fluttering
Their fins, shivering. A chill breeze
Shaking out clouds like nun's habits.

In minutes the miraculous dusk
Has become clammy, umbrellas
Of white wool round mastheads.
Visibility is down to a cable.

And we are left with the bleating
Of sirens, a whole convoy
Scattered like toys thrown down
By some petulant child, haphazardly.

Waiting for it to clear,
Anchored, one becomes aware
Merely of black looming
And fading, the great cliffs

Of bows that any second
Might split you, clean
As a fish, between lighting
A cigarette and inhaling.

J.W.51B

A Convoy

From the Supplement to the London Gazette, 17 *October* 1950:
"The conduct of all officers and men of the escort and
covering forces throughout this successful action against
greatly superior forces was in accordance with the tradi-
tions of the service. That an enemy force of at least one
pocket battleship, one heavy cruiser and six destroyers, with
all the advantages of surprise and concentration, should
be held off for four hours by five destroyers and driven
from the area by two 6-inch cruisers, without any loss to
the convoy, is most creditable and satisfactory."

The sea, phlegm-coloured, bone-white, fuming.

And Poulson waddled crabwise to his Action Station
And Smith wrote home on thin, ruled paper
And Wilson read Spicy Stories in his hammock,
And Reeder, McGregor, Wood and "Blood" Reid
Played Uckers on the tea-wet, tilting table.

Bulkheads sweated, steel shuddered, silence grew.
A cockroach plopped, fat as a plum, on Dyson's lip.

A week out of Iceland, nosing the Barents Sea,
And guns were trained hourly to prevent freezing.
Snow on the ladders and life-lines, Jesus Christ
In the person of Torpedoman Jones, bearded

And tense as a Da Vinci, suffering from shell-shock.
A dropped spoon jumped him to Heaven.

Escort of six destroyers, the convoy fourteen
    merchantmen,
Carrying tanks, stores, artillery, Murmansk-bound.
Onslow, Obedient, Obdurate, Orwell, Achates,
And sailing from Scapa in a Force Seven gale,
Bulldog, damaged, turned back, *Achates*
Sprang her foremast, and *Oribi*, with Gyro failure,
Lost touch, making her own way up.

Destroyers were the same again in ice,
Raked silhouettes in crusted overcoats that cramped
On guns and bridge. The look-outs stamped,
And into messes water seeped.

December the 24th, oiling at Seidis: and Watch Ashore
Went ashore, walking the pink inlet
In search of canned beer, silk stockings, and a bit
Of what you fancy, which was not there.
White muzzles of the fiord, hills of sphagnum.
And the trawlers like foals nuzzling the oiler.

C.O.'s at conference, and anchors dragging,
While Masters spoke up for their limitations
And Captain (D) cajoled them to keep station,
Knowing the obstinacy of their independence,
How they liked to make the most
Of it – how it got them lost.
Charts were studied, and the screening diagrams
For *Circe, Ledbury* and *Chiddingfold,*
Whose job was to round up stragglers, laid down.
In the NAAFI Butcher and Bredon to keep warm

Danced with each other a mock hornpipe, and a sour
Putty-faced girl stood staring with a plate of cakes.

At 2300, when at home trees were being
Laden with presents and last year's Father Christmas
Was buttoning his duffle and seeing
Beyond the mineswept channel that one face
Warm on a pillow that trailed
Hair through dreams of reunion, they sailed,
Line abreast and making thirteen knots,
Visibility three miles, to O, the appointed spot.
Meeting the convoy at which place,
Circe and her sisters left them.
And on their own, into a head sea now,
Waves like tissue paper on every bow,
Erratically they pitched on a course of 320,
Yawing and rolling plenty.

Hammocks swinging as the sea swings,
  Creaking and straining and sly.
    One bright eye
Perpetually open, a smoky fever
Of dream in the lamp's shadowing rings.
    Some dreams are for ever.

And Tanzie Lee dreamed of St Anthony's choir,
And Ellis of the Jig and Tool ads in the *Argus*,
And Bennett of Pusser's Stores and what he could win,
And Totman of Tottenham Hotspur in the good days,
And the Buffer of feeling a woman in various ways.

The Log Book written on a tilting desk,
Records a position at noon on the 26th
Of 68° 23' North, 6° 32' West,

And the welcome sight of a Catalina.
Winds freshened, and at gale force
The convoy to 071° altered course,
And the big ships, their Marines
With more flannel than a Pusser's blanket,
Swung at familiar moorings.

Regular as a metronome,
The arc of roll, rolling them away,
                    Away from home,
Though home is where you make it,
On a hard locker and a blanket,
As the bulging hammocks sway
And the darkness turns to grey,
                    The grey of day.

On the Twenty-ninth the trawler *Vizalma* hove to,
A merchantman shifted her cargo, speed was reduced
To six knots, and course again altered.
The convoy, neat once, faltered
In formation. 21, unable to keep her
Station, hove to. *Bramble*, a minesweeper,
Was sent to search for three
That were missing. *Oribi* was absent.

We have a good chance, the Captain
(D) had said, of getting through,
Days being so short, and the crew
In the messes on Christmas Eve, writing letters,
Had paused, and without disrespect made
Obscene gestures, cynical about the degrees
Of comfort administered by gold braid.
But, trusting that there were better
Times ahead, since they could not be worse,

Had strewn the air with flowery curses,
What might pass for thoughts, unsaid.
Whether they had yet been spotted
Was now for each the relevant
Question, framed on waking
To the bosun's mate on his way round shaking
Reliefs, surfacing in damp fug
To a reality they could not shrug
Easily off. Thoughts were painstaking.

Had they? Possibly, south of Iceland,
By a Focke-Wulf, while *Obdurate* obtained
Contacts and dropped depth charges,
And alarm reports came in from Norway.
But nothing definite save mess-deck buzzes
Travelled through frozen spray.
Huddled on "B" Gun, furred as a husky,
Roley Wilson dreaming of the sun,
A great one for Tombola, dwelt upon
Those green calm nights and that
Auspicious occasion when Doctor's Chum,
Number Nine, and Royal Salute, Twenty-one,
Came up to win him the House,
And the sun liquified, quiet as a mouse
The sea, and all night in,
After the Last Dog, he cuddled his money.

Each man waiting was two men,
The man with Pay Book and number,
A rank and a duty, Sick Berth
Tiffy. Torpedoman, Tanky
And Stoker, and another man inside
With a healthy fear for his own skin,
Reading month-old local papers,

What the Stars Foretell, the News
Of the World in which he was scarcely in,
Except by proxy. These two
Travelled a parallel course,
The man of ice outside,
The dreaming man within.

No longer comforting planes or the friendly gulls
Garrotting the sky and dipping their wings
In salute or farewell. Not since Jan Mayen,
Passed to port a day or so back, had the sea
Done other than boiled, hissed, spewed
With emptiness, rattling its boredom from horizon
To horizon, something none would ever again want
    to set eyes on.

Next day, the thirtieth, noon, ten were present
Of the fourteen, *Vizalma* catching up
And the Commodore increasing to nine,
Then slowing to allow stragglers to return,
Obdurate hustling them in on the first
Fine afternoon when ice could be chipped,
A smile be made without lips freezing.
And Captain (D) at 1630 saw slipped
Into formation the last of his charges,
Observing the crisis approach like a doctor
His patient's temperature, reckoning the chances,
As now between the ice and German Norway,
South of Bear Island, he felt his way.

Final dark, convoy and escort aware
Of each other, not knowing their relative
Positions, but simply that somewhere
Each followed a similar course,

A helmsman bringing the wheel to midships,
Steering 090, wind force 3,
North-westerly, and sixteen degrees of frost
Hardening on the steel deck, radar
And Asdic and RL 85 slowly revolving,
W/T silent, gunlayers solving
Hypothetical problems, and the hammocks
Settling in a subsiding swell.

Dreams were dreamed, as well
They might, of child and grate,
Of eyes opening their lashes
To meet their own, holding steady
That for which some were not ready,
Some were already too late,
And chided themselves, men with no
High opinion of their own behaviour,
But belonging somewhere, belonging,
Inarticulate even in their longing.

Courses crossing, like lines on a hand,
Darkness disintegrating, and throwing up
Into the net of the morning, like fish,
A stranded sea of vessels, ignorantly
Approaching, British and German.

II
Not dawn, for dawn means light,
And from this light sun was withdrawn,
But eventually it was not night
Any more, and a sardine-coloured sea
Tipped into clouds torn
Here and there, the dull grey
Glinting, as if turned to metal.

And *Hyderabad* sighted them first,
On a bearing of 180°, two destroyers
She believed to be Russian
So did not report, her captain
Being of a trusting nature,
And they continued awhile, until *Obdurate*
Closed them, and was fired on,
The enemy retiring to the north-westward.

And, ahead, in *Onslow*, Captain (D),
W/T silence now being broken,
Signalled his destroyers, Join Me,
My course 280, Speed 20,
And the destroyers, breaking
Out of line, heeled over,
Increasing revolutions, like the spokes
Of an umbrella being opened,
Spray icing the look-outs,
Forming up in line ahead.

On "A" Gun Smithers, settled behind
The gunshield, shook from his eyes
Pieces of dream, the unkind
Sea walling him in, spattering the wrists
Lately in fancy she had kissed.

In the engine room Stoker Davies
Of Merioneth said Hell loudly,
Giving all of the six l's full value,
And wiping his hands on waste,
Unctuously as a stage doctor,
Fussed over his gauges, proud as if
Playing at Cardiff Arms Park,
The eyes of all Wales on him.

And *Onslow,* with *Orwell,*
Obedient, Obdurate taking up station
Astern of her, ordered the Commodore
East, an emergency turn
Of 135, *Achates* laying smoke between,
And they closed the enemy.

Northward, an hour distant, Burnett,
Flying his flag of Rear-Admiral (D)
In *Sheffield – Jamaica* in company –
Turned on a course of 170,
Making haste to that grey
Chessboard of ocean, on whose invisible
Squares ships related
The possible to the impossible.

Now in *Onslow* was sighted to starboard
An unknown vessel, approaching at speed,
Opening fire on *Achates* with six-inch guns;
And *Onslow,* altering to a parallel course,
At a range of 9000 returned her fire,
Identifying the enemy as the cruiser *Hipper,*
And made ready torpedoes, which *Hipper,*
Declining to receive, retired from
In smoke, desultorily shelling.
Which was the decoy, *Hipper* or those
Other destroyers, now numbering six,
That lurked in attendance, like
Male nurses round some gross invalid,
Expectant yet afraid?

More than one course was open,
But Sherbrooke, preying on the enemy's
Fear of torpedos, pursued him,

Orwell astern, ordering *Obdurate*
And *Obedient* back to the convoy,
The best he could do for it
In the way of defence, while he himself
Went after *Hipper*, peppering her,
Tracers like bridges of fireworks
Linking over distance, and the slow
Grey swell heaving itself up,
Collapsing and breathless.

Hipper and *Onslow*, sea-horses
Entwining, as one turned, the other
Also, on parallel courses
Steaming, a zig-zag raking
The forenoon, as two forces,
From each other breaking,
Manoeuvred for position.
Like squids squirting their ink
In defence, ships smoked sky
Round them, camouflaging.

Herringbone waters, and the cold
Drifting south, narrowing
The escape routes, icing breeches;
A slow confetti of snow
Made bridal the gun teams,
Aiming awhile their dreams
At the blizzard of *Hipper*.
Who rounded, small flames
Pricking her, the stronger
Animal, able no longer
To stomach indignity,
Firing broadsides on *Onslow*.

Onslow to *Obdurate*: have been hit
Forward and in engine room.
Onslow to Obedient: Captain (D) wounded,
Take over for time being.
Onslow to Rear-Admiral (Destroyers):
Am retiring on convoy making smoke screen.

Onslow to *Obedient*: Forward Magazine
Flooded, fire in boiler room.
Am proceeding to southward of convoy.

The lamp flicked out the messages.
While below, on Port wave,
A Leading Telegraphist gave
Such information to Murmansk
As was necessary, repeating
To Force "R" what was relevant.

And *Obedient* took over, *Onslow*
In flames retiring, relinquishing
Seniority, a private ship
Fighting her private battle.

"A" and "B" Guns unable to fire,
Radar destroyed, aerials ripped,
And, forward, the sea stripping
The Mess decks, spilling over tables,
Fire and water clinching like boxers
As the ship listed, sprawling them.
Tamblin, his earphones awry, like a laurel wreath
Slipped on a drunken god, gargled to death
In water with a noise of snoring.

Slip, slop, slip, slop, a boarding house slattern
In carpet slippers answering
The door, a telegram from 5 Mess
Refusing to come home, Gone Whoring
After a sleazy mermaid with tin fins,
Eyes rheumy with salt, shins
Barked on a stanchion, a pattern
Only too familiar, only this time
It was for good, not evil,
That the old devil
Was absent, and it was the sea
Slip slopping, no woman, over his property,
Ditty Box, Taxi case, bag and hammock,
Glazing his eyes under whose lids
Passed no parade of marriage,
But the sightless accountancy of one
Shocked out of debt, owing no one.

Ammunition party hurled into attitudes
Of early morning after a wild night,
Smith going for'ard trod and stumbled
On Aistrop's belly, which forever rumbled,
And now put him off balance,
Its last chance at assertion.
Passing buckets, not the buck,
From hand to hand, and heart to heart,
"X" and "Y" doors clanging shut,
And merciful Arctic sliding at last
Its cold arms round the flames.

The human chain bent, passed,
Bent, passed, bent, passed,
Simmons forgetting his fibrositis
And Donkin, his four-eyes swept overboard,

Entered Heaven in a blur,
Which was as well, for little was left of him.

Mess traps banging, with a double issue
Of rum to all hands, ignorant
Now of the situation, apparent
Or real, but at all events
Warm, hearing steel shudder,
Noticing movements of rudder,
While smells of anaesthetic
Seeped for'ard, an Arctic
Stew was served of spuds
And corned dog, and the First
Lieutenant's voice coolly organised
What needed to be organised,
As if it was Sunday Divisions
And the Base Captain was coming aboard.

So *Onslow* rejoined in falling darkness,
Having aided the elements' cancellation
Of each other, fire and water
A litany henceforward for all
Who had use of litanies,
Her captain sightless in his sea cabin,
Having ordered the battle, wounded
As Ahab, and no less dogged.
Smythe, a C.W. candidate
With an eye on the future, smoothed
His beard, felt his neck
To confirm it was still there,
And ventured on deck,
Having a mind to recapitulate
The action, test the weather,
And generally nose out the future.

He saw, as he held to a ladder
For support (the angle of list
Being forty-five degrees), *Achates*
Laying smoke astern, though holed
Forward, once more straddled
By *Lützow*, now up in support
Of *Hipper*; and slowly,
Northern Gem taking off survivors,
Doing the obsequies, she sank.

He saw, the convoy steaming sedate
As swans on a river, his own ship
Flying pennants of smoke,
Obedient and *Orwell* and *Obdurate*
To port, from time to time
Making sorties on a horizon
Of gunflash, returning to the rhyme
Of escort after passages of free verse.

And he learned soon how *Sheffield*
And *Jamaica*, surprising the enemy
On their disengaged side, had set fire
To *Lützow*, and finding fine
On the bow a loafing enemy destroyer
Had incidentally removed it –
A salutary lesson, inflicted
With the minimum of effort
And a courteous lack of ostentation
Entirely in keeping
With the traditions of the Service.

Beneath the ice-floes sleeping,
Embalmed in salt
The sewn-up bodies slipping

Into silent vaults.
The sea of Barents received them,
Men with no faults
Of courage, for the weeping
Would be elsewhere,
Far from its keeping.

Seamen of *Onslow, Achates,*
Travellers without warrants or visas,
It was All Night In
On that long Watch that encompasses
The Dogs, the Middle, the Forenoon,
The Morning, Afternoon,
And First that shall be the last,
That shall be forever.

A sea littered, and *Onslow,*
Collision mats in place, holes stopped,
Leaning on a falling ocean,
The wind dropped
As if not to disturb the dreaming
Of blanketed Wardroom forms
Gently up estuaries steaming
Bearing no names.

And the Buffer would remember
The date, the Thirty-first of December,
When the forward fire
And repair party disintegrated
Before his eyes,
Leaving him an undelivered bottle
On his hands, an expression of surprise
That remained there for days.

Heads floating like lilies,
Pulled under by currents, or surfacing
To take no part
In the tactical situation,
To appraise which was an art
Dependent on survival.
This water-garden of the foc'sle,
These statues of the heart.

And if you had brought
To the attention of Dinwiddy,
A three-badge A.B., notorious
For the kindness of his soul,
The foulness of his language,
His captain's intuitive appreciation
Of a situation fraught with ambiguity,
Six enemy destroyers off the starboard quarter,
A pocket battleship and a heavy cruiser
Approaching on the port bow,
And the necessity of drawing fire
Away from the convoy, yet not deserting it,
His head would have reeled,
His tongue licked out obscenities,
His heart hardened, though even as
He blasphemed, simulating fear,
And voicing the popular opinion
That for a destroyer to engage
An eight-inch cruiser was a form
Of insanity credible only
In one wanting a double layer
Of scrambled egg on his cap,
He would have grown most
Marvellously cool and unfussed,

As loyal to the concepts
Of sacrifice and duty
As to his often, and fastidiously expressed,
Devotion to his own self-interests.

For the ears, the thud of gunfire,
The thunderous shudder of impact,
The hissing of charred wood,
The clanging of steel doors;
And the faint voice of the Gunnery Officer,
Relayed over earphones,
"Short" – "Over" – "Straddle",
The thin bird-cry of a man
Pinioned under shells, and the endless
Injections of the surgeon.
For the nose, smell of burning,
Clove sweetness of anaesthetic, the acrid
Odour of cordite.

For the eyes, smoke
Stinging, disarrangements
Of the familiar, Rita Hayworth
Stripped from a locker lid, dice
Rattling in a tea cup, and Reid's
Severed arm cuddling a hammock.
The slow grey heave of waters,
A Focke-Wulfe cruising,
Predatory as a shark.

The cold seen almost as a colour
– Ice-grey, gelatinous, glass-edged –
And that rose-shaped explosion of fire,
Booming over bruised sea,
Which those on deck or bridge

Saw as either doom or rescue
And had to guess which.

Enemy withdrawn, and convoy
Proceeding to Kola. This night
Of New Year, sea moderating,
Darkness scattered its largesse,
Though the close escort, not
Knowing the enemy's movements,
Had small feeling of escape,
Merely of being afloat,
Of inching forward into dawn,
Eastward round the North Cape.

Course 226°, Wind Force 2,
And at noon, on January 2nd,
Position 69° N, 35° 30' E,
Land was sighted ahead.
The convoy in three columns,
White Sea to starboard,
And nosing through fog patches
The minesweeper *Harrier*, in company
With two Russian destroyers,
Joined on the port beam.

Kildin Island, and *Seagull*
In position, Syet Navalok Light
Blinking its welcome that spelled
Quite simply "It is over
For the moment, you are half-way
Home, you are half-way".

And *Obedient* leading,
The convoy, in line ahead,

Slipped down the inlet behind her,
Onslow already along side,
Having discharged her wounded.

From snow into snow. A kind
Of deliverance, an unloading.
As skies, snow-heavy, are lightened
By the falling of flakes, the mind
Also is eased of anxieties.
The rattle of anchors, whiff of fish,
And Lyons, after a run ashore,
Tucking in the ears of his Rabbits,
Or so he imagined himself,
Gazing at low hills like snow-clouds,
And snow-clouds like low hills.

Arrived, the deck stationary, bulkheads sweating.

Stained and wet as shot rabbit
And his eye clinging to a thread
Like spit, a bullseye that might
Be swallowed whole, taking sight
With it.
   Hiding his forehead
He picked his way from the bridge
With the indifference of a waiter.

We found him hours later,
Bolt upright on the edge
Of his bunk two decks below,
Eye dangling like a monocle, face like snow.

Landmarks of sorts there always were,
Flamborough Head, Immingham, Southwold—
Sea-marks as well, the buoys
Marking the channel where E-boats,
Engines idling, waited for us, all contacts
Muffled. But they were mere signposts,
Not aspects of arrival—

No, the real landmark that made
The pulse quicken, coming up on deck
On a summer morning, was the black
And white pagoda of the Trinity House
Pilot Station, exotic to us as Konorak
Or Madurai. Anchoring there,
We could look down from above
At the launches swishing up the estuary
With signals and mail, Wrens at the helm
In bell-bottoms, their lovely hair flying.
It was the nearest we ever got to love.

We fished him from the sea, eyes blurred,
And dripping. Stripped him, gave him rum,
Then hauled him like a prisoner to the dock,
Asked questions gently, kind. Playing dumb,
He gave his rank and number, smiled
Cynically as we probed for more. Riled,
Trying not to see his shrivelled cock,
We asked him where he'd laid his mines,
And when he merely said his rank
The captain, as if he hadn't heard,
Inclined politely, murmuring "we'll see to that",
And gave the Chief P.O. dismissal signs.
The Leutnant shrugged "Ich bin Soldat".

Grotesquely draped as though in furs,
His blanket half-slipped across one arm,
He shifted position, uncertain whether charm
And pride were his prerogative or ours.
"All right, Bo'sun, take him below,
We'll comb the area all bloody night
If necessary, and if we should hit
He'll be the first to go,
Can't be helped, sorry and all that".
So we marched him below to the stokers' flat,
And altered course out of the zone,
Steaming in circles until his nerve broke
And he asked to come up and explain
The pattern of his mines "for everyone's sake".
By dawn our sweepers had got rid of them all,
And we sailed up the Schelde as if on a lake.
Troops followed us in; it was quite uneventful.

She was usually good for a fuck
If she liked you, or just felt
Like a change from long hours
At the bar at the mercy of bores—
She'd flick you a look, then turn on her heel,
Legs in black nylon the colour of rail,
Making for the shed by the siding
That backed on the quay. Soon you would feel
The hardening thrust of those low-sliding
Breasts as she pressed and then knelt
As she liked and bucked as you felt
She was starting to come. She'd wail
Gently, straighten and then tuck
Her blouse back into her skirt, kiss,
And, slightly unsteady, trot her way back,
Humming. You marvelled at your luck.

Better than to scorn is to bless
Such promiscuity, the "angel of Harwich"
Who made love as a nurse
Might minister to the suffering, eyes
And legs wide, but with so rich,
So tender a compassion only fools would despise.
At sea, it was her you'd most miss.

Sometimes, miles out, you get
A sensation of land, as if somewhere
Deep down a valley was surfacing—
The sea seems to heave contours
Of green out of itself
And you watch fields and forests
Being salvaged like wrecks.

I imagine a man whistling
To his dog, someone pruning shrubs,
The sounds of a cricket match.
A pub door shuts on faint music.

It is just such fantasies that mean
England is not after all
A figment of our deprivation,
But a landscape with outriders
Bringing real consolations.

Indigo dusk. Stokers, wiping grease
From their fingers, take the night air,
Throwing waste to the gannets.
Indiscriminate in their appetites,
They dive, as deprived as we are.

II

Post-War

Ochre sea, the Quai des Pêcheurs awash.
Through loops of your hair, sails
Drip heliotrope, cinnamon, rust.
Beyond the lighthouse the breakers crash.

In bed we are warm and entwined.
For this it was all worth it.
We shed war like our clothes,
In each other are confined.

SENGWARDEN BARRACKS

Something (but what?) could be made of this,
Two U-boat officers turning to piss
In swastika shapes against a wall.

These level fields are Wehrmacht grey,
Friesians chew cud all the way
To the Baltic, camouflaged as pillboxes.

From the barracks a horn gramophone
And Ilse Werner singing *Abends*
In der Kaserne, a long way from home.

Here gold eagles rust like the sky.
We paint out glory and forget how to fly.

Like a crow's foot the clenched rock
Of this island obliterated by our bombers.
Circling it by gunboat, we critically take stock.

It stinks of decay, fishy and fleshless,
And most of all here, in cattle-like pens
Where U-boats fetched up for repairs, breathless.

A catacomb of tunnels hidden from the sky,
Where a navy famished for fucking
Once fertilised it, drained it dry.

Now even fishing boats, red-sailed
And cadaverous, give it a wide berth.
Flotillas of gulls peck its churned earth.

Only what is useless – guns, shelters, equipment –
Has survived, one with the cormorants
Bloodwinged in sunset and bestial as the Mitchells

That flattened this outpost of fishermen and shells.

White boats on the Alster like confetti,
Slate sky, and a sense of diminishing
Returns, the handcarts smaller and emptier.

Women have cloth faces, will exchange
Anything for anything, though in St Pauli
Wrestle naked in mud during dinner.

As you watch them, children grow thinner,
Their eyes huger. Is it for this we came,
To go whoring and give defeat a name?

BRIDGE PARTNER

In memory of Lieutenant-Commander R. Chesney, R.N.V.R.

This man with huge belly and gold earring
Through black whiskers produced a high whinny.
He murdered twice. Now he's my partner
At bridge, a Commander with a penchant
For finesses. He's costing me a fortune.
He makes psychic bids and has pig's eyes.

Generous with loot, he passed on
Krug by the caseful, arranged girls
(His own tastes ambiguous), fixed transport—
Himself riding a Mercedes, waving through cheroot
    smoke.
His was the way of the conqueror, if only
It could last! But he died by his own hand,
Bankrupt like the rest of us, Nemesis upon him.

Padre, I have seen you haggard
After breakfast, pale grey with hangover,
Yet impressively upright, wearing
For our benefit, your fragile parishioners,
A brave face, though we're mostly past caring.

What, in God's name, can you say to us,
Assembled before you, officers and ratings,
Caps off and dressed in our best, shifting
Restlessly, only longing for gin?
A gust catches your surplice, you spin

Violently and I think you're capsized.
I can't hear a word that you're saying,
But no matter. As in battle, all the sustenance
We need pours forth from those eyes,
Sea-blue and bloodshot, that have saintliness incised.

FRÄULEIN

As for my predecessor,
Leutnant von R, whom times have laid
Aside, you mend and press
Uniforms. On request, undress,
Share the bed you made.

As for my predecessor
You came, in a manner
Of speaking, with the room.
We both got a bargain.
Neither can complain.

DEMOBILISATION

The entered world is like a sleep,
But men the self-same vigil keep.

The future offers dreams of pleasure,
But can we now employ our leisure,

Or have we let this fragile art
Become a spectre in the heart?

The river's limpid line surrounds
The dwindling morals and the grounds

On which we start afresh to prove
The valid images of love.

The pencilled eyebrows of the face
We gaze at conjure with the trace

Of familiar and objective fact,
As shadows merge into the act.

And we are half what luck contrives
In our one or other lives.

The house, whose wings glowed white in heat,
Had shutters through whose slits the striped
And ochre river dimpled into fields of wheat.
The mud flats and the natives gave a look
Of coiled repression and of power
That always stuck – a legend in a book.

Time sifted the images, yet humiliating things,
Like falling fortunes, lingered to remind
– A chance remark, a suicide,
A door one dared not look behind –
Reappearing in sleep, a false world
With dreams mysterious and deep.

But they no longer mattered or disturbed.
What occurred in the billiard room,
The nursery at night, or at the river's edge,
Were sooner or later, by experience, curbed,
Though the most serious repression
Was glossed over and remained unheard.

The smell assaults you first, from places
Where nightly the padded steps rehearse
Africa's movements in its restless sleep.
Here all our captive faults are nursed
Brooding in their sultry paces.

Like phrases they turn and reiterate
Lost meanings in their striped and alien cages,
Pausing to blink a heavy eye at sun
That curls the pallid ends of pages
In their history blanked-out and done.

Now nothing in their world remains
Where always on a straw-laid floor
They meditate, like prisoners in a war
Fought for lost causes, whose mere act
Of living forced them to participate.

Ignorant of ends and means, knowing
Only the blank reality of exile, they seek
The one vivid proof of life, their shadow,
That alone answers when they speak –
A familiar whom, a little way behind, they tow.

Watching, we turn our backs and move away,
Suddenly ashamed and moved by some glint
Of pity in their shooting eyes, as if to-day
They showed some symptom or some hint
Of our predicament to-morrow, or the next day.

At night the Front like coloured barley-sugar; but now
Soft blue, all soda, the air goes flat over flower-beds,
Blue railings and beaches. Below, half-painted boats, bow
Up, settle in sand, names like Moss-Rose and Dolphin
Drying in a breeze that flicks at the ribs of the tide.
The chalk coastline folds up its wings of Beachy Head
And Worthing, fluttering white over water like brides.
Regency squares, the Pavilion, oysters and mussels and gin.

Piers like wading confectionery, esplanades of striped tulip.
Cricket began here yesterday, the air heavy, suitable
For medium-paced bowlers. Deck-chairs, though, mostly
    were vacant,
Faces white over startling green. Later, trains will decant
People with baskets, litter and opinions, the seaside's staple
Ingredients. To-day Langridge pushes the ball for unfussed
Singles; ladies clap from check rugs, talk to retired colonels.
On tomato-red verandas the scoring rate is discussed.

Sussex *v.* Lancashire, the air birded and green after rain,
Dew on syringa and cherry. Seaward the water
Is satin, pale emerald, fretted with lace at the edges,
The whole sky rinsed easy like nerves after pain.
May here is childhood, lost somewhere between and never
Recovered, but again moved nearer, as a lever
Turned on the pier flickers the Past into pictures.
A time of immediacy, optimism, without stricture.

Postcards and bathing-machines and old prints.
Something comes back, the inkling, the momentary hint
Of what we had wanted to be, though differently now,
For the conditions are different and what we had wanted
We wanted as we were then, without conscience, unhaunted,
And given the chance must refuse to want it again.
Only, occasionally, we escape, we return where we were:
Watching cricket at Brighton, Cornford bowling through
    sea-scented air.

Rain, rolling up eastward from Bristol, hurried
After the train. Travelling towards you, I watched Bath
Struck by swords of light, their long hilts buried
In cloud. And over Chippenham felt, like an aftermath
Of quarrel, the thunder ease its torrents
Over the Avon, drenching the valley in scent.

Driving from Swindon, the downs that armed off
Your childhood, riding over Martinsell, hair flying,
Were blanketed; mist rubbery over Oare, drying
Out where Gopher Wood, Marlborough, Huish reached
Upwards from Pewsey and the roads, like bleached
Tongues, lick at the high ground above Salisbury.

June in retreat, the grazing landscape
Of canals and stone bridges now camouflaged in mist,
Self-protective as at the approach of invaders, summer
Buried for later. Near Ogbourne wet roads twist
Past camps, out-houses for manoeuvres, rich fields like
    capes
Slung over their shoulders. Rain beats like a drummer.

Neat country, where even the woods skirting
The Kennet, lime trees and elm, beeches like tight curls
On the swell of Savernake, seem planned – Nature
    flirting
With Time to connive at gracious estates –
Upavon, Stonehenge, Avebury, dripping stone
Like a measure, hardening the soil to a plate.

But back where the bare chalk swings
Out like a sail above Draycot, gull-white on rings
Of coarse green, the rain leaves us – darkness hurrying
Over Devizes, Alton, West Stowell, the sky bruised violet.
Summer calls up its stars, Cygnus, Cepheus, Hercules,
Draco and Ursa, straining night through your trees.

The real inciters are never seen – they exist
By imaginary need or whispered orders.
And fed through channels of petty adventure,
These half-grown men riot, till one of them is killed.
Then causes evaporate; just the dead persist.

Water towers; the river; the golden tombs
Of Kadhimain; and wider, beyond the city,
Circles of green with fountaining branches
Of leaves and dates. Sand craters, like bombs
That have missed their mark, lie out in trenches,
   Where the tilted wingspan
Of sight crowds the whole town to an entity.

But the view is deceptive. We struggle
For poise in the air, and leave in our slipstream
Hills starched under snow, the straggle
Of huts round the river; and sun like a cream
Melting over palaces. Pipelines tell us more,
   Lining the Tigris with money,
Heaping promises like sand, and, as easily, war.

Not that poverty means happiness,
The picturesque past something to look back
On with credit. But now, as glittering and less,
Bagdad flashes its *arriviste* suburbs
Under us, elbowing out villages, the lack
   Of a synthesis grows brutally
Evident. Ignorance and greed futilely trying to tally.

And what we see here, a fragmentary
Culture unwrapped on an auburn morning,
Its legacies of luxury, squalor, and unnecessary
Suffering, ought to remind us – a warning
Against digging our toes in, overloading fate
   With avarice; till, forced to it,
Mobs move on us, like great rivers in spate.

The stages can all be seen, rubbed clear of their dirt –
At first only crude but wonderful mosaics, the clumsy
Efforts at communication, where writing is simply
A bird or a tree, with words whose curt
    Meaning comes from an alphabet
Entirely pictorial: the pure draughtsman's intellect.

Then, later, embellishment; chalices and figurines,
    women
And men portrayed as their genitals. Snaked rings
Symbolishing ritual, and bellams whose curved prows
Paraphrase travel. Carved scenes emphasising
    Luxury, feluccas and dhows
Flushed in the sunset of more finished specimens.

But, mostly, the glazed pots and bitumen bowls
Convey only essentials; details were regarded as rhetoric,
Decorations superfluous to their necessary roles
Of enlarging awareness. The real achievement
    Of these fragmentary, written-on relics
Is immediacy, their beautiful economy of statement.

The Dove with its silver eyelids climbs and turns
      Through parabolas of blue
          The whole sky
             Askew
And behind us the pipe-line stretches and burns.
      At intervals oil is ignited, fire
          Burning off gases
             Below
As, air-bound, we alter course northwards and feel
      Persia like a crust rising
          To meet us,
             Snow
Now the route we fly over and probe like a weal.

Parks takes ten off two successive balls from Wright,
A cut to the rhododendrons and a hook for six.
And memory begins suddenly to play its tricks:
I see his father batting, as, if here, he might.

Now Tunbridge Wells, 1951; the hair far lighter,
And body boyish, flesh strung across thin bone,
And arms sinewy as the wrists are thrown
At the spinning ball, the stance much straighter.

Now it is June full of heaped petals,
The day steamy, tropical; rain glistens
On the pavilion, shining on corrugated metal,
The closeness has an air that listens.

Then it was Eastbourne, 1935; a date
Phrased like a vintage, sea-fret on the windscreen.
And Parks, rubicund and squat, busily sedate,
Pushing Verity square, moving his score to nineteen.

Images of Then, so neatly parcelled and tied
By ribbons of war – but now through a chance
Resemblance re-opened; a son's stance
At the wicket opens the closed years wide.

And it is no good resisting the interior
Assessment, the fusion of memory and hope
That comes flooding to impose on inferior
Attainment – yesterday, today, twisted like a rope.

Parks drives Wright under dripping green trees,
The images compare and a father waves away
Applause, pale sea like a rug over the knees,
Covering him, the son burying his day

With charmed strokes. And abstractedly watching,
Drowning, I struggle to shake off the Past
Whose arms clasp like a mother, catching
Up with me, summer at half-mast.

The silent inquisitors subside. The crowd,
Curiously unreal in this regency spa, clap,
A confectionery line under bushes heavily bowed
In the damp. Then Parks pierces Wright's leg-trap.

And we come through, back to the present.
Sussex 300 for 2. Moss roses on the hill.
A dry taste in the mouth, but the moment
Sufficient, being what we are, ourselves still.

Diagonally
        across this plush green square,
                centre of a village,
Cricket ground, short-cut from farm to house,
Axis on which the Downs sail their trees, cutting
Their chalk cliffs away sharp as bowsprits,
And off which a duckpond carries the fluff
Of clouds as well as thistle, reed and tiger lily—
The elms now
        thrust
           their masts in shadow,
Dew dampening under foot, apples red as cricket balls.
Doves gargle in the beeches
As August subsides on these acid hills:
Clayton, Ditchling, Plumpton, Westmeston,
A green weal crimped out of over-rich soil.
Farm and fruit country
           poorly veined for ore,
Without deposits, save for the joke bones
At intervals dug from the dykes round Lewes,
But land for men's eyes, fields for perpetual awakening:
Summer-soft, river-tongued, bereft of cities.
The coast only has its rind of development
Seaford, Peacehaven, Telscombe – the muddled
Gift of northerners with a taste for penitence.
This field is mid-Sussex,
        the centre marked by a tree,
             a windmill,
Whose still sails denote stability, a point
In time that remains constant, landmarks
True as the points of a compass—
Cold Harbour, Ringles Cross, Five Ash Down:

On this common, imagination and memory meet
Where signposts lead to my childhood,
A rosegarden and a top-heavy lake,
Ardingly,
                Balcombe,
                                rabbit woods of Highbrook,
Slopes my child in his turn climbs tomorrow.
Leaves fall, kites of rust plunging the blackberries
And the mist forms like a smoking tyre
Round copse and churchyard. The tombstones smudge,
Beard, Tidy, Mears, Wickens, good local families
Love-locked in death, arms about each other;
And the greenflies crawl across the moss, picking
At leaf and flower. Sun with an echo of bells
Night-washes the Ouse, gone to seed here,
"River" too grand a name for its miry stagnance.
Autumn it is
                Sleevelessly thrusting
                                us back to our capitals,
Centres of responsibility from which, over our shoulders,
We glance back through the ringing mists, the smoke
Of bonfires, at what we have made of summer,
At what this fixed landscape, our own, has made of us.

Quartered and tilted
As on a quarter deck, segments of wheat below,
Arrangements of flax, and, fine of their bow,
The sea, these smooth hills sail quilted
And patched, the sun on their axis.

Aiming east–west,
In autumn, as for harbour, with russet flags dressed,
Beeches in headwinds streaming, their contours rest
On each other, surfaces spiked with tree-rings,
Dented with dew-ponds, and rolling at moorings

Like camouflaged Carriers.
Chocolate-furrowed, blond, a watered-silk green,
Mount Harry dips, then climbs to the Beacon,
And the windmills on Clayton, like warriors
In armour, raise vizors to try out the weather.

Once sheep-belled, but arable
Now, these escarpments so soft under cloud,
Move on the summit like a planchette table,
Guided by currents – or seem to, loud
Winds buffeting their chalk prows,

Jet planes circling
The blue, as if coming in to land,
Like the larks, with a mere folding
Of wings, a flurry of greensand.
So clear the landmarks, so true the bearings,

That although everything
Here seems buoyant, to float on springs,
It gives off at the same time an air
Of permanency; to be fair
Even when unsettled, to be stationary even as it swings.

III
Home and Colonial

Poem, shut the window, turn the gas on yourself,
Be a footplate man, a Liberal who retains his deposit.
Get psittacosis, commit adultery with an M.P. on the
    divan,
Break the sound barrier, engineer strikes and riots.
Poem, bowl out the Australians, announce a £30,000
    transfer,
Record the gossip at a deb dance, the malice at a
    couturier's,
Elaborate the sex-life of film stars, the plunging
Necklines of the heroines of T.V. Poem, climb
    mountains,
Have quintuplets, split the atom, or celebrate your
    diamond jubilee.
Take part in one of the many Fancy Dress Balls of the
    Century,
Inject horses, blackmail a peer, penetrate the Iron
    Curtain.
Draw forth a joke from the P.M., walk off the Q.E.
Slash taxes, put up the price of bread, murder your wife.
Be an Abstract of a poem, show your legs like a starlet,
Praise the hardships of the conquistadores of the
    household.
Be a dietician, a Teddy Boy, a racing motorist.
Give to the National Trust your baroque battlements,
Solve crosswords, win Pools, get a psychiatrist
Crossed off the register for unbecoming conduct,
    disappear
Like a diplomat or get your hair bleached
To seaweed under the drier and sue for damages.
Be for each man the image of his desire,
A Beauty Queen, a Tournedos Rossini, a Hawker Hunter,

For a woman a mink coat, a washing machine, a Latin
 lover.

Poem, cure poliomyelitis, baldness, and man of his
 avarice,
Investigate the wage-scale, the cause of prostitution, the
 decline of the family,
Poem, be news, vulgar and to the point, otherwise
No one will take any notice of you, you will decay
Like a returned Empire builder, a retired soldier, the
 muscles
Of a middle-aged oarsman. You must take a hold
On yourself, read the ads, go in for courses
That will make you respectable in high or public places.
Poem, forget tenderness, let loose your pent-up savagery
On images that will make the compositors bleed from
 ear to ear.
Stand up for yourself with a good grace – for you will
 need it.

FOR A LONDON CHILD

For Jonathan

Sleep where the plane tree nets you with shadow,
A geranium like a lamp at your elbow.

Sleep to the rocking rhythm of trains,
To the scent of petunias blooded by June rains.

Sleep by a sea of asphalt, rubbery with heat,
Where people's voices are stones thrown from the street.

Sleep in dreams whose glances are all loving,
Now when the clock is steady, before the hands start
    moving.

Sleep to the query of dogs, muzzles glinting like metal,
Whose own mouth knows only the breast's white milkfall.

Sleep now, wool mariner, on waves of content,
Admiral of innocence, scrutinising and silent.

Sleep where green leaves feather the stone
Urns stained by winter, falling for you alone;

Who wait your first winter, child still cocooned
From cold, a half-sketched poem, mandolin not yet
    tuned.

Sleep in your image of sailor or poet, explorer,
    engine-driver,
· Child of two kisses, on your brow a four-leaved clover.

STANLEY MATTHEWS

Not often *con brio*, but *andante, andante*,
    horseless, though jockey-like and jaunty,
Straddling the touchline, live margin
    not out of the game, nor quite in,
Made by him green and magnetic, stroller
Indifferent as a cat dissembling, rolling
A little as on deck, till the mouse, the ball,
    slides palely to him,
And shyly, almost with deprecatory cough, he is off.

Head of a Perugino, with faint flare
Of the nostrils, as though Lipizzaner-like,
    he sniffed at the air,
Finding it good beneath him, he draws
Defenders towards him, the ball a bait
They refuse like a poisoned chocolate,
    retreating, till he slows his gait
To a walk, inviting the tackle, inciting it.

At last, unrefusable, dangling the ball at the instep
He is charged – and stiffening so slowly
It is rarely perceptible, he executes with a squirm
Of the hips, a twist more suggestive than apparent,
    that lazily disdainful move *toreros* term
        a Veronica – it's enough.
Only emptiness following him, pursuing some scent
Of his own, he weaves in towards,
    not away from, fresh tacklers,
Who, turning about to gain time, are by him
    harried, pursued not pursuers.

Now gathers speed, nursing the ball as he cruises,
Eyes judging distance, noting the gaps, the spaces
Vital for colleagues to move to, slowing a trace,
As from Vivaldi to Dibdin, pausing,
        and leisurely, leisurely, swings
To the left upright his centre, on hips
His hands, observing the goalkeeper spring,
        heads rising vainly to the ball's curve
Just as it's plucked from them; and dispassionately
Back to his mark he trots, whistling through closed lips.

Trim as a yacht, with similar lightness
        – of keel, of reaction to surface – with salt air
Tanned, this incomparable player, in decline fair
        to look at, nor in decline either,
Improving like wine with age, has come far –
        born to one, a barber, who boxed
Not with such filial magnificence, but well.
"The greatest of all time," *meraviglioso*, Matthews –
        Stoke City, Blackpool and England.
Expressionless enchanter, weaving as on strings
Conceptual patterns to a private music, heard
Only by him, to whose slowly emerging theme
He rehearses steps, soloist in compulsions of a dream.

All afternoon in a borrowed flat
Staring at a stained ceiling,
He wondered if what she said
She was really feeling
"Without you I am dead"
And how long it would be like that.

He raised his wrist behind her head
To seek the watch-face in secret;
She, stirring beside him, murmured
"Don't keep looking, it's not time yet"
Making him smile, like a child caught stealing,
But pleasureless at time's freewheeling.

Touching her eyelids, brushing with his lashes
Her cheekbone, he felt ritual first splashes
Of tears, caught up on her lips
Absorbed by his finger tips:
Always it would end like this,
The drained immediacy of the kiss.

Traffic outside, light ebbing through curtains
Half-drawn, the ceiling losing its stains
– Contour of guilt outstaring his face
Breasts to his breast, she and he in this place
Belonging to neither, loth in the groove
Of satiety to have to make the first move.

Thus would the pattern be—
Till one, hankering again to be free,
Became evasive, such regretful, such tender
Excuses, he praying for another to befriend her
And she – should it be she – pleading a
Family's unhappiness, that others were needing her.

And watching their diagonals narrow and cross
Both would assent; even that one whose loss
Was the greater, seeing the future take
Inevitable shape, more readily for the other's sake
Would affirm "My darling, I understand, I swear"
Knowing understanding impossible to bear.

Pedalling between lectures, spokes throwing off
Sun like Catherine Wheels, the damp grass
Bestowing its sweetness from a long way off
– When perhaps the Australians were playing
On a May morning – he might class
As lacking sensibility, swaying
Down the Broad between family saloons, those
Who, with heads like his own humming
Black tunes of Baudelaire, money-box Cantos
Clinking from Pound, did not also hanker
As they rode, gowns lateral, for the drumming
Music of the Parks, his magnetic anchor.
Arrived, would he settle (as earlier
Before the laughterless sweep of the *Fleurs
Du Mal*) to marvel at technique exercised
For propitiatory sakes, the surlier
Humours exorcised by purity of stroke,
As of language – an innings by McCabe packed
With epigrams, Bradman ruthless as if sacking
A city, but appropriating to himself
By his mastery anodynes to nostalgia—
"Pick, pack, pock, puck", Joyce's "drops of water
In a fountain falling softly in the brimming bowl",
A boundary, whose grouped trees might have been
Set up by Claude or Poussin for their own
Remedial passion – and settled, discover the green
Circle splashed by moving white, the honey
Of the bats, would remain as fixed in the mind
As ever Baudelaire's spleen, Pound's semantic
        notions of money.

At night, above the mauve stocks' capture
Of the dew-close, lower air,
They straighten – as it were, tall
Debutantes freed at some summer ball
Of too-short escorts – trailing
Through ash-blue, thin and falling
Sky layer after layer

Of scent. On gangling stalks
Green rises like soda into the five
White petals, suffusing where clusters fork
From the stem. And the scent, more possessive
Than fruit, has about it a sovereign
Confidence, at first a tang,
Then precisely that odour of a girl's skin
On which balms of expressed love hang.

TOBACCO PLANTS

At dusk, they come into their own,
Exchange familiarity and the dusty
Endeavours of the long day for that feeling
Of excitement working girls communicate
When at last, dressed for a date,
They shake off utility, undergo sea-change.
Now they expand, set senses reeling.

A peculiar expectancy, half serene
Half restless, seizes them.
Sap rises like soda suffusing their five
Petals, green bubbles that sieve
Scent into whiteness, aromas more possessive
Than anything dabbed from a bottle –
An exhalation of fragrance spilling from the fork,
Part caress, part throttle.

KOALA

For Victoria

How should I describe you – eternal
Image of the cuddly bear, solace
Of your button-nosed familiars of every race,
Who on cold nights or those long cheerless
Afternoons, when to be small
Is to be misunderstood, clasp your toy belly and kiss
Injustice away – whom to possess most surely is to miss.

Drawing your iron-bark claws along my wrist
You narrow two rheumy eyes where indifference
Has laid a deposit of pink mist –
Your hold on life so delicate,
That to lessen those twin and absorbing opiates
You live on – ladles of sleep and of eucalypt,
Storehouses of bored over-intelligence

Into which you continually dip – would be to remove
For ever the Empire's one pure Existentialist.
Fatalist, addict, catalyst
Of early but enduring emotions, you lay like a glove
A clenched fist over mine, twitching a tar
Nose as if it was snuff not gum leaves you sniff –
Crybaby, as passive as a teddy, you simply *are*.

And restoring you to that high fork
In the tree where the juiciest morsels bunch,
I watch you pluck with the tiniest tremble a stalk,
Thrusting the gum sap home with a crunch
Like the breaking of celery, passenger to oblivion –
Perfervid muncher, whom tomorrow I shall come upon
Sun-doped and happy, a gnawed twig in your paw like a
    pen.

The sky rinsed as a blue-jean collar,
And the train, on this April Monday, idling,
With nothing better to do than to follow
The curves and windings of sidling
Rivers, and, sniffing marsh air, at snail's
Pace clank through the flapping
Washing, proud as *Potemkin* –

Swans glide in flotillas on lapping
Waters, and the estuaries hang up their sails,
Indigo, rust and cerulean,
And clouds, like transfers, soak
On surfaces of inlets where beached boats
Vamp the sun on a morning that floats.

Hamble Halt, Bursledon, Bitterne –
We edge through rushes, inhaling the paint
From upturned houseboats, ketches, yawls,
And hear soon the first faint
Siren notes from Pompey harbour – the train crawls
Past old Landing Craft, their flaking keels
No longer chipped after raking patrols,
But flopped on the mud like veteran seals.

And I am suddenly returned there,
To a crumbling shore and a barracks where
– Was it in the same lifetime? –
We dawdled between ships, without rhyme
Or reason filling in each day,
Awaiting the signal that would sever
The links, and whisk us from the bay
For an unknown time that might be for ever.

Bailey bowling, McLean cuts him late for one.
I walk from the Long Room into slanting sun.
Two ancients halt as Statham starts his run.
Then, elbows linked, but straight as sailors
On a tilting deck, they move. One, square-shouldered as
    a tailor's
Model, leans over, whispering in the other's ear:
"Go easy. Steps here. This end bowling."
Turning, I watch Barnes guide Rhodes into fresher air,
As if to continue an innings, though Rhodes may only
    play by ear.

They huddle in groups on shingle, aiming
Bows bearing loved names – Tiger, Seashell, Deirdre,
The Fifteen-Two – below railings that flake
Paint on them, lack of light maiming

The whole coastline. Under tall seas creaming
Mauve-green, seaweed, like ribbons from straw hats
Worn by girls in Victorian pictures,
Strews a beach still emptily dreaming –

And the boats, paired for comfort, sad shapes
Beneath dwindled tamarisk, wear salt
Along gunwales, thin coverings like capes
Drawn in a taut line from stern to stem.

Gulls screech from the pier, from stained cupolas,
Snatching wet bread flung by blue-jerseyed men,
Braced against breezes, who take small steps
By their boats, ten paces east, then west ten –

The names a kind of mnemonic, Deirdre, Seashell,
Maria – waiting to reinhabit them, to come alive
– Boats, men, at a standstill – till one day summer
Suddenly floats them, buoyant as sea-swell.

The softening of her face which comes
At only that moment
– Eyes hazing over, lips more oval,
And the skin bruising with blood
Like sea over coral –
Is an image of what happens
At precisely that moment
When the poem, taking leave
Of its poet, glides
Down the slipway, at last free;
And absorbed in its journey,
The union of bow and waters,
Writes its last lines alone.

After love, to continue the caress
Is both to insure
Against sadness and to reassure
The one and the other that "Yes"
Has not become "No",
And the urge to get up and dress,
Leave a kiss on the brow, and go,
Is one that will subside
In the slowly returning tide
That brings to the next caress
True elements of tenderness.

I listen to your heart,
That part
Most difficult to own,
Or yet disown.

The laws it follows
In its breast-dark hollow
For all I know,
Or you allow,

Relate to tides.
You may be drawn
By movements of the moon
To others' sides.

The ocean-tasting limbs
Spilled now across this bed
In other curtained rooms
Are spread

With the same naturalness
As do some confess
Misdemeanours without query
At the least inquiry.

But remains apart
The non-committal heart,
Beating more or less
In pleasure and distress.

Waking, she saw on the chair
The clothes of the man beside her,
Trousers, shirt, vest untidily spilled,
But into a shape that was vaguely human;
And being that kind of woman,
Asked herself what kind of man filled
Them, a question she could not answer.

Leg-spinners pose problems much like love,
Requiring commitment, the taking of a chance.
Half-way deludes; the bold advance.

Right back, there's time to watch
Developments, though perhaps too late.
It's not spectacular, but can conciliate.

Instinctively romantics move towards,
Preventing complexities by their embrace,
Batsman and lover embarked as overlords.

Always the first to fall,
Like gay girls who cannot resist
The loosening effects of the sun,
But must themselves be undone,
Girdle-free, rolling on grass,
They are plundered by small
Pert birds who, gripping the flint wall,
Have waited for just this
Opportunity, and pounce with sharp kiss
To the core, shaking
Waferish beaks, their eyes tight shut
– As a man does, first thing,
Sluicing in cold water –
Their summer thirst almost past slaking.

IV

In Africa

DANDY IN ELOFF STREET

With fawn fedora and a rolled umbrella,
Palm Beach suit and co-respondent shoes,
He eyes himself in dummy-grinning windows,
Smiling when his image in the plate-glass does.
Creases sharp as razors, but avoiding ladders,
He prowls up Eloff on a short-term shadow.
His teeth are gleaming and his tie is yellow.
The outer man on show, the inner one lies fallow.

Arrogant in his fancies, building castles
In the air, he scrutinises finger nails and whistles
Softly to himself (as if all that matters
Is precisely how much cuff exceeds the sleeve).
Yet, behind smoked lens, his bloodshot eyes are eagles,
Swooping insults up from looks of red-necked betters.
His nostrils sniff out scorn, and, flaring, leave
A trail of wounded self-love like a spoor.

Chest puffed out, a nylon pigeon, his lips are bugles
Blowing fanfares of his pride from door to door.
Yet, salesman of himself in imaginary encounters,
Randy dandy on the loose from rancid shanties,
He draws out self-respect, instalment by instalment,
Spiritually bankrupt, though a strolling millionaire.
At home, the suit hangs up, still bluffing its
    contentment.
Below, its owner sags; the dandy is up there.

This Bantu on a bicycle racing the sunset
Carries on his shoulder, like a rifle
At the slope, a torn umbrella that
Would pass no sergeant. He will get wet
Anyway, or, if storms fail, will stifle,
For townships are hot. But, unfurled,
His gamp waves like a shield, his hat
Squashes his ears and, sodden, his vest
Takes like a transfer the sunset's medals,
Saffron and crimson. The last burst now, he pedals
As if announcing the end of the world,
Which event alone might curb his unrest.

You have black eyes,
Four years of age,
A chic, cast-off coat
– pepper-and-salt, double-breasted –
A label naming you "Mohammed",
Some slippers, a squashed felt hat.
Nothing else. And "nothing" means just that.

This camp is your home until – well, until.
A flag flaps on a hill.
The *oued* soon will be dry;
Do you know how to cry?

Smoke curls from the tents
Where women who are not your mother,
Hennaed and trinketed, cook.
Your eyes see but do not look.
And men who are not your father,
Turbaned and burned, sit stiff
In rows, like clay pigeons, on a cliff.
Targets do not easily relax.
Your hair is fair as flax.

Guns rattle the mauve hills
Where the last warmth spills
On villages where once you were
One of a family that died.
Not much else. Just that.

You pull down the brim of your hat.
Who knows what goes on inside?

Gold stars on cobalt more alluring than money,
Cool skies of mosaic, and, outside, the glare,
Quivering off courtyard walls in honey,
Beams from a minaret stair
That spirals over swept carpets
Of pale sand.

        Emerging, shoeless on straw,
I catch in a glass door
A stranger's glimpse of my face – eyes jet,
Nose inquiringly aimed, beard
Dark on an old wound, but flawed
White at the impact.

        It was as I feared,
A face in which everything warred,
Indulgence, compassion, sloth, vanity,
Which, brooding on this walled city,
Mosques flashing like cataracts,
Seemed epithets fair to it –

        A casbah-oasis,
Cluttered with camels and carts,
Noising its amusement, once loved,
Where, despite the evidence, men's hearts
Held the same hopes, the same hunger for prophecy.

Whiteness so white here it enthralls,
Whiteness of sails and walls,
Sea-salt and soda.

Yet everywhere touched by gold,
Minarets and beaches, the old
Palaces, young skins.

And blue like some lotion
Of heaven on mosque and ocean,
In assassinating eyes.

A conjunction of colours to blind us –
Yet running me through
At every step with reminders
Of hair that was gold, skin white, eyes blue.

It is a form of absence mainly – of sorrow
And regret, those indulgent aftermaths
Of passion or the event we borrow
From to go back and explore –
That is abroad on this trap-door
And goat-shaped island, tethered
To the desert; where it would seem
Neither passion nor the event
Ever took place, though one can't be sure.

But so idly does it swing,
As if emptied out, at its moorings,
That whether they did or not, Nothing
Has survived, as something positive,
A deposit almost alive,
Cruelly crawling the floor of old eyes –
These blanket-draped Berbers, confident
That lack of a past gives
An edge over history, a right to disparage.

Low hills of Guellala, squat palms
Pitting white beaches ringed by a sea
So buoyant it thrusts to the surface
Its whole content, jewfish and bass,
Mullet, umbrina and sponges,
Embarrassing by their plenty –
As if nothing so easily come by
Could be of account, unlike looks
With their irresolute meanings, their ambiguity.

Yet even indolence, though left in perpetuity,
Exhausts; and at nightfall the Sfax-bound
Mahonnas, prows lisping through bruised sea,
Sails fluttering, curve themselves free
Of a place where only rarity or difficulty
In handling – as here water,
That soft-voiced commodity,
Camel-drawn from wells – interrupts the ritual
Of idleness, makes addicts of them all.

A STONE'S THROW

Choose a stone with a polish
As smooth on it as an olive,
Wrap it carefully in vineleaves,
Take aim, and throw;
On whom it lands you will bestow
The indestructible flavour of yourself,
Which nothing will ever demolish
No matter how bitterly each grieves.

The limp palms coated with dust.
And the coaxed horses, thin about the rump,
Swishing at flies, A stink
Of cigars and dung, through which,
Oily and lubricious, tussore taut over plump
Thighs, women talk as they stalk.
Elaborate this language of the eyes,
Such as belongs to the once-veiled, ink
In their glances, an ambiguous communiqué
Meaning everything or nothing.
                    In the sandhopper paddock
The Favourite balefully urinates, steam
Rising from fizz. On tall heels,
Hair marbled under nylon, metallic legs gleam.

Movement and pecuniary lust,
Where the expense-account faces, olive-smooth,
Suggest what cannot be transacted, a mere
Flicker of eyelids in exchange of prophesies.
And each on his way rejoicing,
Binoculars slung, a gloved woman hung
At the elbow, as if the real purpose
Were social. Silks opening and closing,
A conjuror's slick shuffle, and a hooped
Outsider snaps the fan into focus, nosing
Through the dust.
                    High on the neck, French-style,
Oblivious jockeys goggle at the sun
In a murderous finish. Meanwhile,
Unobtrusively, elsewhere, real murder is done.

Across Bab-Souika at midnight
A switch clicks, throwing a bright
Square on my cracked wall.
There, presently, two shadows fall,
Merge in shadow play, and kiss.
From my bed I watch all this,
The outlines changing, clothes undone,
And, inevitably, the two-in-one.

A snap of shutters, and then spill
Their low and curdling laughs across;
I make a third at the window-sill.
Striped by slats their bodies toss
And flash, nakedly exclusive.
I grow conscious of the stone floor,
The Greeks stertorous next door,
Their crude slumber complacently abusive.

END OF A WAR

The time when it all ends
Returning enemies to friends,
Turns also friends to enemies,
Replaces old with new treacheries.

Lovers alone are honest in their lies,
Others must depend on spies,
Emissaries or go-betweens, whose lives
Depend on ambiguities.

Today a last cortège and ceremonial drums,
White flags fluttering in the blue,
But who any longer believes true
Peace with a cease-fire comes?

The afternoon cloudless, hot, quiet,
As it had been for days
(Though of course, there were always
Noises, harvesters climbing the hill,
The crackle of stubble, apples plopping,
But simply they didn't impinge),
When out of nothing a jet
Low overhead came screaming,
And the blue like silk tore,
Silence after it dropping.
Lying, half-reading, half-dreaming,
I was pitched to an open boat,
Bullets spattering his shoulders and throat
As the plane turned idly away,
That one, not this, on a similar day.

An old terror, long since scotched,
But in its wake others came screaming
And as I sat up and watched
My son playing, suddenly he raced,
Without warning or looking,
Over the lane and, for a split second,
Until he was over, the thought
Came to me, this has been always
How it happened, nobody looking
Or thinking or doing anything
In particular, one of those hot days,
Blue skies, harvesters and stubble,
When IT happens, and the bubble
Bursts, and we are not asleep,
But what happens, happens for keeps.

Asphalt through green, the road
Is open behind and ahead,
The car too, cruising at fifty,
Dusk sifting the hedges
    And the sulphurous
Air subsiding, gone flat
In the musk that hits us,
    Cowparsley and mossroses,
Again sentient, nosing the verges.

Open country, known like a hand
Held often but rarely examined,
And in my reflector the view
Continuing behind, though new,
    Seen the other way round,
Disconcerting – a defiance of logic
That asserts we cannot be both
    Going and coming,
And must look one way at a time.

Villages in evergreen moorings,
Spatters of corn, and now the sky blurring
And deepening, so no more
Can be gained from the mirror.
    I switch on the radio,
Relax. But soon, closing up fast
Behind me, headlamps tearing
    My Indian-inked mirror,
A car I had given up for lost

Miles back in the traffic,
Dazzles and blinds. We resume the old frolic,
Two magnetised cars whose drivers
Once at some lights exchanged glances
        And were indestructibly
Linked, though often obscured
By intruders or darkness,
        Or simply the recognition
That elusiveness, disappearance from view,

Were laws of the game.
I slow, and she does the same,
Her pale hair illuminated
By headlamps whose flames
        Bore at my back
And burn. I smile, while my foot
Depresses the pedal. At eighty
        I finally lose her,
Though her profile pursues like a song.

There's nothing to look back for.
Ahead salt air, the great paw
Of black hills. A horn moon
In blue velvet whose softness
        Both warms and traps –
We share these still. Yet my eyes
Over and again stray to the mirror,
        Drawn by no image
Save recurrent blanks only I recognise.

Raising my pen to put a point
On the page, a dot over an i,
An unsteadily veering fly
Collides in a three-point landing, and settles.
Then, as if carving a joint,
It carefully sharpens its legs,
Sitting up the way a dog begs.
I notice a wing shed like a petal.
It has come here to die.
And my dot, streaked now with blood,
Turns the colour of mud.

V

North from Sicily

Air is what we fly through, scarcely that. Nothing
Is more like it, but over mountains, under cloud
   clothing.

Walls like splints wedge cracked hills zigzagging
To summits bearing crosses or castles with roofs sagging.

An island of alive gods and goddesses, saltcrusted, where
Arabs left fountains, Normans cathedrals, Bourbons their

Decadence seasoned with avarice. I look down
On Palermo, carboned by crags, where once Nelson,

Doting and enslaved, nodded off while she gambled
Far into morning. These vapour trails, scrambled

Over Etna, haze the confetti of boats.
And leaving you I'm caught suddenly by the throat,

The treachery of absence so drying that cold
Pellegrino even finds me parched, while gold

Domes, cloisters flash under me, and I'm utterly strange
To this island's last shot of almond and orange.

SYRACUSE

Her way of walking, light in a halo on hair,
The stained burned backs of legs that climb the stair,
Are holds on time, keeping me rooted there
Whose roots are distant. The bay smudges
To saffron. Plane trees, linking their dark edges,
Fluff themselves out on water. Sirens blow,
Hailing the *Carthage* to Tunis, *Nettuno* to Bari.
These are the essentials, all I need to know,
Looking from my bed, head on left elbow,
The sun beating on stone, on the mainland quarry.

These are, with pen, ink, your body, real;
The rest – coins, statuary, the baroque – no longer
    living,
Except as the present reproduces them, the diving
Boys escaping their broken Greek familiars, a heel
Or arm or genital missing, the women washing
In the fountain, blouses bleached like sails
Over breasts the Museo leaves unhidden. Splashing
Below me, girls squeeze shirts into pails
The colour of sunset. Fishing boats trail
Slug-like wakes from the *piccola marina*, waves
Petering out where the plane trees' shadow
Nets them and lobster pots dredge the sea's graves.
This is a stone island, vacant of grass, of meadow.

Ortygia. Greek columns, a theatre, and old
Dionysius lending his huge ear to whisper of slaves.
The city is caught at the throat by water,
A slim bridge hoisting the suburbs, cement gold
With low sun, squat, ugly and everywhere flatter.

Only these granite peaks stabbing the dusk
With waterless spite retain hate,
Though bells waft there, a musk
Of melon and forgiveness, and a cassata sky
Receives admissions that need never be too late.

All day, on seats along the curved Schiavone,
They move their glittering Coca-Cola tops
As draughts about mosaic boards, whose stony
Surfaces are polished by the mops
Of early-morning cleaners. Roughly a bony
Hand pushes its tinny piece to some new square,
Or eyes lift to S. Giorgio Maggiore, green against the
    copper air.

Outside churches, in drowsy piazzas off the Grand Canal,
Or on small campos that are never quite banal,
Urchins play a kind of bowls with rubber heels –
Though lacking bias, these drop true – in place of
    woods.
Soiled notes change hands depending how they fall.
Cool nuns and scurrying monks peer out from hoods
To note the winner, whooping as he turns cartwheels.

Beneath the clock tower where two Moors
Of enviable muscle strike the hours, green-baize
Tables glow inside saloons with swinging doors.
White cats on window-sills in sun raise
Quizzical whiskers as a shot is missed,
Or narrow their pupils to judge when balls have kissed.
Inside, light smokes on skulls, on ivory, through
    persistent haze.

The ideal city? And, nearby, the ideal
House, scooping the sun from every window
As it planes along competing views –
Four landscapes with dark trees in shadow,
A plain of light where winding waters fuse.
Perhaps. But should we ever slip the Past,
Exchange the lover's for the husband's eye,
Nailing our colours to this Euganean mast,
How long would it extend the real?

The right size, certainly, this watermarked city
Sweltering on its mound, slack streets like ropes
Hanging and notched with pocket palaces,
Thin alleys where athletic cats run races.
And everywhere the stamp of columns, thrust
Of towers, whose bells rock against the slopes
Ringing the valley – woods black below, and rust
Blown on the beech ridges. Perhaps too pretty
For comfort, for wear and tear? It depends who you are.

An austere town, all the same, aware of precise
Limits, careful of over-indulgence and always
Slimming away the fats of development.
A model of timing – conception and achievement
Seeming to be identical, a matter of a few days.
But ideal? Possibly for the withdrawn, the wise.
Yet the rest of us, frail and inconstant, fearing most
That mysteries should vanish, eyes or *ambiance*
Surrender their secrets, might suddenly be lost.

Your hair that makes the most of vines,
Blue shirt against the trellis, and goggles,
Like insect's eyes, reflecting the lagoon.

That's all the Kodacolor yields
To which I add a table
Where Negronis glint, a liquid air

That melts between view-finder and the view.
The lap of gondolas, of subdued jazz,
Great domes that squeeze the sun,

The biscuit palaces, exist without,
Beyond the edges of the fading print.
It was a time of meeting elsewhere soon,

Of brief goodbyes in golden afternoon.
I look again and feel the first
Faint smears of rust in autumn's deadly tune.

There is no blood to point the wound.
Nor where I drag myself along
A spoor such as dying animals show.

I would be happier if there were;
Instead I carry in my head
The stain that marks and slows me so.

But laying your hand against my heart
Can murmur "there" and gently press
Your fingers, repeating softly "yes".

The signs are of a bad day. Before waking
An apprehension of disquiet, premonition of shaking

Foundations, of shaking itself. Yet dreams were real
And rejecting morning the attempt to re-feel

Whomever may seem secure, postpones the dread.
Two hours salvaged from the dead.

Later. An aura of bruising, tongue
Like a caterpillar, a hollowness of lung.

A lurching day, from oasis to oasis.
Oh well. First brandy, soothing of crisis.

Plainly enough, the sky with scraps of blue
Exists. Bars, taxis, newsprint, you.

You. One brandy is not going to do,
Not this time, let's settle for a few,

A round figure, a half-dozen. Better.
The image finally of the given-up letter

Arriving at last. The whole alphabet.
Trembling into focus, the trickle becomes a jet.

What's happening? After all, nothing's wrong,
Nothing to get hold of, only the song

Has an ominous whine, played at the wrong
Speed. So wrong recurs. Can we prolong

What's between us, intoxicant
Of which these six brandies are poor variants?

You've come a long way (they said).
I had a long way to come.

You are fortunate not to be dead.
My home was no longer home.

This has happened to others before.
The door is still ajar.

You could have been killed in the war.
I thank my lucky star.

The music is beginning to flame –
It comes from afar.

That's no kind of question. It's
A matter of timing, of what fits

Two moods, two moments. Meanwhile,
Imagining your profile, am able to identify style,

Consistency of shape, and the fluency of line
That celebrates this one life out of nine.

But you are –
Yes, I am.

DEAD RECKONING

We proceed by dead reckoning,
Without aid of stars or navigational
Instruments, an altogether
Hazardous business. Regardless of weather,
Merely set courses, measure
Off the days, and hope for landfall.

Were either blown out of true,
Mistaking the estimate, we might
Sail indefinitely, night
After night alone. But bearings
Are correlative, courses reciprocal,
So soon we'll be able
To refute what we're fearing.

Plump, pop-eyed, sweating,
His paws keep up their beating
On coarse wood. Wine at his elbow
Is coarse too, but palatable as he follows
The cards, luck advancing or retreating.

He wins more than he loses,
It is not of great import, nor does
He make it appear so. He chooses
To dissemble, though dissembling is unnecessary,
His emotion aesthetic, purely anticipatory.

Later, mopping his brow after midnight,
He walks quiet streets, home past illuminated
Walls, basilicas and towers striped
Like his shirts, black on white.
He enjoys his inheritance of this Renaissance city,
That Botticelli wife, conniving at being just pretty.

There is something of the stork
About her, those kind of calves –
Though when I watch her walk
I'm not sure whether "stalk"
Isn't the image that bears leaves.

Either way, the prevailing colour
Is pale, whiter than sun or gold,
Ash or an alloy beaten and old.
Blonde is too positive, too yellow;
What is intrinsic to her is pallor.

It is that which in this Roman sun,
Among hot eyes and lips, the glare of columns,
Singles her out, *Inglese*, as one
To whom coolness is endemic, any appraisal
Of her renewing, like a fountain's rise and fall.

Gone, and in my driving mirror
The taxi rattles you from sight.
Already I experience symptoms
Of withdrawal, the terror
Separation flies like a kite.

Passegiata, and hot Romans hurrying to *pasta*,
Piazza di Spagna littered with tourists.
But the flowers give off fumes,
Not fragrance, and banks,
Barred like corseted matrons, loom.

Our flagrant white square is a tomb.
Poor Keats. No *aperitivos* for him,
Nor a human mass which stinks,
Either. This *seicento*, chariot of doom,
Is only fit for a midget.

Under a sky etched out in inks,
Dark urine and rose, a fidget
Of wind flaps girls' skirts,
– An image that hurts –
Ripples white shirts.

Past Piazza Navona, heading south
Towards Gaeta, I drive
With hood down, my mouth
Tasting dusty, of your mouth
And ashes. Symptoms of withdrawal,
Like being buried alive.

THE ITALIAN STYLE

A matter of elision, the low
Sweep of eyes and hulls over lengths
Of chassis, elegance of *gran turismo*.
Space can't interrupt
The bonnet's snubly abrupt
Flow, its masking of strength.
Spinnings of silver in spoked wheels,
Exhaust-throatiness, sleekness of seals.

A continuation of women
Whose legacy of antique carriage, the urn,
Allows that swivel of the hips
While heads remain level, lips
Preparatory of darkness, eyes of black milk
Engaging as they spurn.
Legs fade into secrecies of silk
Too delicate for the opulence of hair.

And even here in the south
Where resentment shapes the mouth
Like a lipstick and the baring
Of full breasts under black cotton
Holds a tenderness akin to swearing
– the harsh syllables sluiced with spit –
Poverty has a style, *un perfetto bilico*,
Its adherents recognise, dying from lack of it.

Even at 1/500th you can't freeze him,
Make his image quite static.
He remains more mobile than diagrammatic.

Take compass, protractor. However
You dismantle him, the parts
Remain true, suggest velocity.

Leonardo would have made him fly,
This batsman so revving with power
He seems airborne.

Like some prototype birdman
Straining at silk moorings, he conveys
Ambiguity, both imprisonment and release.

Never mind the earthbound heaviness
Of hip, of shoulders, his cover-drive
Evokes airiness, an effortless take-off.

A study in anatomy, circa 1930. Anonymous.
But there, nonchalantly stuffed
In his pocket, that blue handkerchief signs it.

It is, after all, a kind
Of music, an elaborating of themes
That swell and subside, which
In the converting of open spaces
Take on a clean edge.
    A throw, a chip,
A flick, Wilson to Charlton,
To Moore, to Hunt, to Greaves –
The diagonals cross, green space is charmed.

A precise movement, balletic in ordained
Agility, with the players as if magnetised
Moving into places seemingly allotted them
– They seem from above to be pushed like counters
And only the fluffed pass, the momentary
Crudity disconcerting as a clerical oath,
Destroys the illusion. A goal restores it.

Arms raised like gladiators, they embrace.
Human emotions swamp them, childishly even
For such protagonists of perfection.
    And involved in this mixture
Of the fallible and the dreamy,
The percussive and the lilting, they demonstrate
How art exists on many levels, spirit
And matter close-knit as strangling lianas.

Dilapidated Greek crow, subfusc
And shabby below the morning glories,
Astride the banana leaves or tittuping
Like a half-pissed lawyer between jacaranda
And frangipani, bougainvillea and plumbago
You simulate great age, wreak
Private havoc with your black secateur.

Penitent in your tailcoat, venerable
Dud waiter or clerk in failing chambers,
That shutter of an eye, flickery
As *cinéma bleu*, makes baleful apology
For a morning of shit and extravagance.
What you haven't knocked off bears
No mentioning. You're in your element, old
    gammy-leg.

You're one of the family now, alert
For privileges (and don't you show it),
Blasphemous as a bootlegger at breakfast,
Stumping around all day, ham-
Acting your injury while the rest of us, stunned
By the heat, marvel at your energy –
There's no holding you, ancient old astronaut.

Yet it's barely a week since,
More dead than alive, you fell
Limp as a shuttlecock on to our terrace,
Victim of overconfidence but certain
Of immortal properties, a special claim
On our sympathy. From a death
To a myth so soon is good going,
Old walking-wounded, old scabface.
Now earn your keep with this poem.

VI
Return Journeys

Swirling angostura over ice
I watch the furred suns fill
The whole window with light
– snow on the Downs packed tight –
The ice in my glass slice
Into shapes, fjord into fjord spill.

It is the same cleft
And glacial view, as looking back
On the rim of the Arctic
I once saw Vatnojökull melt as we left,
Peaks streaked this aromatic
Bittersweet pink, flushing sea irretrievably black.

Smudges of grey on the brown Baltic,
The stone islands come at us, septic
And marshy. And I experience that familiar
Sinking of the spirit, as if treachery
And confinement had smells of their own,
Borne by the harsh syllables of Kronstadt.

Last night we entered the Gulf of Finland,
Coasts snowfree and coniferous, barely recognisable
As that unsmiling promontory, iced-in and sable,
We once slid up on with aircraft and curses.
In the bar, high on cheap vodka, Trade Unionists
Sang the Red Flag, danced if they were able.

Ahead of us a fleet rots in its lair,
Captive of itself, but wrapped in the air
Of an old secretiveness, faith in the protective
Mysteries like a charm on it. Spectral
And anonymous, without clues to identity,
Ships brood in collusion, dissembling as fakes.

On a breeze of ambergris and mud gulls break
From a flat estuary and now, in our herringbone wake,
The batteries disperse. Standing on deck
With my son, half my age then, I pass him
The binoculars that brought into live focus
Those names Sverdlov, Odessa, that seem suddenly
    shrunk.

We enter the canal, rain like soot
Falling. He turns up his windcheater, lapels
A cluster of badges, profiles of cosmonaut,
Lenin, gleaming on damp serge. And precariously seated
On damp railings, binoculars raised, his fragility conveys
The real sense of a circle completed.

Marooned by a downpour we stare
Hour after hour at stills of Soviet epics,
Blown-up and grainy. They are already historic,
These revolutionary encounters, where, smelling like fur
Of wet animals, today's crews take refuge too.
The Soviet Union loves Heroes and huge here
They fire guns or reduced to toys
Give scale to models. It's a Boys
Own Exhibition where everything is true,
Neither enemies nor Allies obscuring the view.

Mooning from picture to picture, these curious
Men, noses to canvas, follow me, the furious
Rain pitting the Neva. They exhale gloom,
Faces like rind of bacon. I assume
Their expression of awe, noticing my own ship,
Wrongly captioned, trailing its carcass
Towards Kola. Perhaps it's a slip.
History has always been subject to bias,
And here what's important is giving a bloom
To sacrifice, ideas a high gloss
Regardless of accuracy. This temple to sailors
Of a fleet more mutinous than deadly sprays
Nostalgia like musk, records no failures.

I dream something knocking in my skull,
Only this hammering's outside. A full
Moon turns old scaffolding blue. All
Is being prepared for celebration, every wall
Lacquered, leaves swept as they fall.

A faint hangover, a faintly sour taste
Predictable after such junketing, such feasts
Of vodka. I stumble in false haste
For the alkaseltzer, reluctant to waste
Any of the morning, its revelatory yeast.

A zoo-like reverberation from the corridor,
The guardian crone established on each floor
To prevent orgy. Snore after snore,
Until gradually the door
Assumes colour and handle, and the poor
Wretch humps bedclothes and dreams into store.

It is 1 a.m., the transit lounge
Freezing. I open *Anna Karenina*
"Happy families are all alike; every
Unhappy family is unhappy
In its own way" but cannot,
Under the gaze of Lenin,
Vast blow-ups of dams and collectives,
Settle to it. My fellow passengers,
Pakistani and Indian, drained of their colour,
Whisper through striped mufflers.

I am going home, if home
Is where you come from. I imagine
The thin rind of orange
That over the Himalayas will mean dawn
And Delhi, drums and desertion.
Half my life ago, in this same snow,
Smelling this same smell of sour bread
And cabbages, I left Russia,
Unhappy in my own way, more eager still for take-off.

The first addictive smell
And that curiously sated light
In which dhows and islands float
Lining the air with spices.

The beginning and end
Of India, birth and death,
The bay curved as a kukri
And on Malabar Hill the vultures,
Like seedy waiters, scooping the crumbs off corpses.

Sometimes at dusk
Returning through lanes heady with hibiscus
We come across groups of cricketers,
Indians mostly, and visible
As blurs of flannel, their high laughs
Skimming the river like silver.

Around us the ibis,
Wounded by sunset, take off
In flocks of vermilion. We pass
Lines of women in saris, melting
Like the sky into velvet. Dogs howl,
And past village stalls
Smells of rum and roti hang on us still.

Half-squirrel, half-rat, but with the incisors
Of the real killer, he has come
Into his own silk empire. In naves
Of cool cane he basks like a voluptuary,
Savouring his whiskers. He is in charge now,
Wet-mouthed addict from whom, like the cutters,
Africa is remote, a mere rolling of eyes.
They have won through together,
Shedding their serfdom. Thus do we see them,
Plush overseers on the crown of the road,
Those nights when we cruise through molasses,
Our headlamps spraying long grasses
That sometimes are set fire to. Homeless,
Then, these rodent police, eyes like paraffin,
Scuttle before us, their empire in flames.

At Mahalibaripuram
There is only the temple
A dead cobra draped on the rocks like a belt
The man having his hair cut
Three women in saris.

The beach runs for ever,
Salt spraying the pagodas,
The lion, the bull and the elephant
Halted in their tracks,
And the stone chariots hub-deep in sand.
The Pallava empire ended here,
Where Durga and the buffalo wrestled
And the hoofmarks of a horse
Cantering along wet sand contract
And expand like the valves of a heart.

BENGAL

Against the betel-stained violence
The senseless murders that appal
The oppression of words and climate
That breathe Bengal

You must set the softness of heart,
A querulous literacy,
And the old ox-eyed gentleness
That rips them apart.

"The hour of the cowbells" is what
These sometimes abstemious Bengalis,
Camped in their homeless dusk

Call that delirious moment
When light melts and car-horns mellow,
And we in our whisky culture

Fret in the traffic, smoke
From the jute mills coating the Hooghly,
Faces like pebbles bleaching the maidan.

It is the moment when saris
And soft drinks, sweetmeats and sweet eyes,
Take on the colour of sunset,

Expresses hooting out of Howrah,
Tent-flaps opening like mouths.

After the long night
Close to each other, their profound
But simple needs met by their mouths
Skilled in such loving, they awoke
To bulbuls tinny as bangles
Sky sliced watermelon.

And taking off
On the long flight to Khajuraho,
Ox eyes like sidelights on runways,
Hills of dried blood,
They still tasted each other,
Felt sky like blue in their veins.

Only at the temples,
Places of greenness and great movement,
Where love was elaborated like chess,
The instinctual given a number,
Did ideas of religion drop from them,
Like sleep from eyelids, sun shut by an umbrella.

It was always afternoon
When we went there, everything in shade,
The palms like splayed umbrellas, the frayed
Banana leaves the same colour
As the bead curtains rattling on the verandah,
My grandmother rocking back and forth.

Huge and handsome, she seemed
Physically as rooted as indeed she was
By birth and tradition, growing
Out of the floorboards like a vast lettuce
Gone to seed, but entirely there
In her frail finery, about her a kind of glowing

Nostalgia that bred images
Of eminence, in which she washed us
As if they were a stream still flowing
—French planters of indigo, Irish colonels dead early
Of drink or dysentery, East Indiamen, judges,
Directors of jute mills, surgeons, burly

Impresarios of the railway, moustaches
Venomous but with a family stutter.
Now at last they had run out, too many
Killed too young, and what flowed
Or flowered were the stains and gashes,
Dry rot in the floorboards where Granny

Pat rocked under the insults of mynahs,
One loopy daughter puffing from a green holder,
Banging out preludes on a tinny piano,
The other, a saint in her way, never back
From tending the backward, and always the smell
Of bananas and cigarettes, poverty growing bolder.

A map of India carved,
As it might be a heart, on the back
Of a cigarette case. In uniform pockets
I could trace the shape of Bengal,
Calcutta alive at my fingertips,
The Hooghly through ice. On deck
After dinner, nights mild or atrocious,
I'd inhale childhood – drifts
From the compound of curry and *pan*,
Smells of the racecourse, betel-stains
Like blood in the speech of bearers—
All that remained to set against drowning,
Tall seas turned on their backs
Like doped tigers, allegiances of the exile
Without family, without family feeling.

The boundaries became wrong, ghosts
Of a forfeited unity, but their fading
Disguised it. The rub of materials,
Naval serge, flannel, white duck,
Had worn out the heart, the old essences
Thinned into nothing. And the case,
Lying in a drawer for years, had lost
Its suggestiveness. Only now,
Coming on it suddenly and carrying it
Back to Bengal, do I feel
Under my fingers like braille
The frontiers begin to come true,
The heart beat from the gold. I take
The case from my pocket and here,

In Calcutta, open it to the air,
Hoping that more will adhere
Than the stew of corpses and cowdung—
Something of the old power to evoke
Images that might last out a life.

I

Night expresses hooting across India,
The clank and shunt of an empire

Outstaying its welcome. I open eyes
To an ayah's eyes, the shuffle of cards.

Coaldust on my tongue like a wafer,
And in a swaying lavatory a woman's

Knees slanting moonlight at her belly.
The engines hiss and spill.

The Deccan moored to huge mango trees,
Mosquito nets like child brides.

Stations are marble dormitories, fruitstalls
Inset like altars, wax dripping –

An air of the morgue, all these sleepers
Huddled like mailbags without addresses.

Dawn of papaya and fresh lime.

II

The burra-sahib dressed as for the golfcourse,
Shorts, suede shoes, sports shirt open at the neck.

Outside, the bearer chews *pan* and betel,
Mouth smeared on the edge of haemorrhage.

Whisky and crime stories, and at halts wreaths
Of tuberoses and marigold, ash ceremonies.

Bottles in a dressing case gaudy as spices
In Bow Bazaar, crushed essences like shut parasols.

The rattle of points and bangles. The air
Is sulphurous, spiralling out of mutiny,

The embrace of miners and goddesses,
Where everything escapes, hands palm upward.

Pink layer of icing sugar,
Till the straw sun dissolves it,
And the Downs, drained by the cold
Of their green, sweep grey
To grey sea. Trees are mastheads.

Elements of blue like eyelids
Open sky clinking iron
With hooves of horses on bridle
Paths, back after riding out,
And the lanes lathered with breath.

As yet it is anybody's
Morning, a slate clouded
With nothing; but gradually,
Under the cold, something's
Moving, beginning to conspire
Towards a finish flushed with silver.

Scoops of mist in hills that swing
And feint away seaward, tweed smudges
Through windscreen wipers, the season
Turning as the Citröen turns to tilt
The mercury of the river, boats
Tethered like horses, horses still as boats.
We pass horseboxes, bookmakers equipped like fishermen,
Shopkeepers in a small way of business
Hurrying through autumn as if it were escaping them.

And a ticket falls from my raincoat
Hidroplanador Macau Para Hongkong
The same kind of day, islands
Shrinking in mist, the South China sea
The colour of the Adur, junks
Scattered like bits of brown leaf,
Paddleboats of the Companhia de Navegaçao Shun Tak
Noisy with whores and booze and music,
Smells of urine and shrimps,
That particular sweat exuded by gamblers.

The old *Taipa* went down,
Turning turtle in a typhoon, and I can smell
The same racecourse sweat now, smoke clearing
To faces yellow over green baize,
As looking from Lukinachow over the frontier
To Red China, fishermen and guards
Patrolling the Shumchun river, the mist
Came up at one, like off the Adur,
Gelatinous, and set in it
Tethered boats, horses, portraits of Mao.

I

The phone rings and I know it's you,
But not exactly who – a dull
And dopy voice with flat sedated lull
Between the static; or inconsequential blonde
Whose tales of orgy, drink or fond
Pursuit of that oblivion just beyond
Belief are rich in misses
Too close for comfort or consoling kisses?

II

I hear the crackling air alive
With those invading eyes your guilt contrives
And wonder which of two, who both
Are on the line today and seeming loth
To let the other speak, will say goodbye,
Penitent or punitive. And when I ask—
Not able to look you in the eye,
But taking your fantasies to task—
Whether you believe a word you say, you reply
Dutifully, no I believe nothing at all,
Suddenly bereft, letting the receiver fall.

III

I wait across a county like a hull
Low down in water, rain a dripping sail,
Then put the specious arguments on view
To make the ward, its wretched crew,
Fade into oblivion. But they'll come back

When I ring off, re-forming for attack,
And then we'll have the same old cycle,
Despair, revenge, the familiar trickle
Of blood or almost overdose. A kind of game,
Only the stakes are villainous and your name
Still fragile: unless you mean to lose
The body and the talent too promising to use.

Field-grey of ghost officers, of survivors,
Black leather in coats swung like opera
Full length with menace, black boots,
Black gauntlets in puffs of dust
Down country lanes, eagles, goggles,
Eyeglasses, iron-crosses, and labourers
With clanking milkchurns and the blank
Surprised look of scarecrows.
After so many years
The country seems curiously tame
And lobotomised, the old
Merely old, the pinewoods cut, lakes dredged.

Recognition has gone out of the eyes
That have become glass, sightless.
They cannot remember the barracks
Nights of conquest, sinkings, song,
A creeper of fog making
Your own memory seem faulty,
Men in white coats with syringes
Taking the pain from futility,
Obliterating the old barracks the old days.

Sailors off duty whistling after girls
In the long evenings corn becoming sea-blue
Milk blondes with milk-blue eyes
I remember the obstinacy
Of spires against gales of watered ice,
Land flattened by Protestantism
Hovering like a smell of old vegetables,
Heine and Heineken, brass bands
And a dog with three legs,

Cyclists with coats open like men
Exposing themselves and nothing to expose.

The landmarks have been bulldozed
Signposts point the wrong way
In housing estates cows are marooned
It is hard to put much face
To so depressing a past, the mirrors
Of lakes empty of embellishment
Friesian girls with legs in black silk
Friesian ports with men on one leg.

Bathing huts line the old quays,
Postcards of U-boats and holidaymakers
In striped costumes – the Kaiser
And blue movies – what remains constant
Are the headstones like fields of green teeth
Shingle and sea flapping like tarpaulins
The land running out running down.

From seas that had been dull
For days, white horses like real
White horses with startled eyes grew
Out of troughs and with slew
And heave of flanks like seal
Or whale the slack liquorice hull
Of a U-boat surfacing. Then
It becomes merely a matter when,
And through the angled periscope who.

YEARLINGS

A string of horses black against the snow,
The December light already beginning to go

And the beeches absorbing them, a rust
Tunnel through which like mist

They jog, shadowy invaders.
Caparisoned, they suggest courtliness

And lineage, heirs
To historic names whose sires

Gaze through hooded eyes,
Still innocent of pride or surprise.

All day they had stood in the heat
Like statues, immune to weather
Or flies, but occasionally towing
Plaster effigies to new moorings.

Then, in the cool,
Powdery bodies striped with sunset,
They seemed to lose patience,
Charging like zebra for water.
And, as suddenly, stopped,
Atavism gone out of them,
But the stream returning their manes,
Clouds racing to dispersal.

The indigo glint of this river,
Bones of Prussian thoroughbreds crushed
To make so pure a blue

And the glint of this Indian
Immobile behind perfectly round glasses
Hooked over huge queries.

I see Gandhi bending over me
A lamp like a halo
And the round walnut skull with huge ears
The glint of his specs in mid-air
Humming like wires

And that day in his museum
Traffic melting in the heat
The case with his specs
And sandals, the assassin's bullet
Like an old filling

Cut-out photographs
With grins curling at the edges
Dead marigolds on black marble
The sickly resonance of hysteria

The glint of this river
Is the glint carried all these years
By Gandhi's glasses bent over me,
The perfectly round glasses of this Indian.

Two nights running in the early hours
I've woken to imagine their footsteps
Echo past the Jungfernstieg. They round
The Alster like black scarecrows flapping arms,
The woman with such puffy eyes
The man in homburg and smoked glasses.

They seemed to swivel with ugly shoos and laughs,
Herding me off the pavement like an animal
Into the traffic. Once vaguely pretty
In languid southern fashion, she smells
Of scent and doughnut, smiles black ice.
His coat is fur-lined, reaching to his calves.

It's hard to reconcile their malice,
Or did I witness once, in squalor,
Their nightly scavenging for rations,
The dustbin trips, like werewolves on the prowl?
Or meet him in his palmy days
A Commandant's corset on his banker's body,
The double-lightning on the turkey collar?

VII

Across America

Between Sepulveda and Jefferson,
I sensed rather than felt
The nudge of the pink Cadillac snout
Angled across us, only at your shout
Saw the drunk face of the gelatinous
Blonde, eyes shut, Marlboro askew on her lip –

It was like yelling through double glass
In an aquarium. She couldn't have heard.
But, tossing her hair, suddenly froze
– her cigarette burned to its tip? –
Into some kind of awareness, like a bird
Swerving at impact, mirror-close.

Sometimes at night her face
Comes at me, a crushed rose
Shedding petals into smoke.
It was the saving grace
Of your presence that allows me to look.

Venice "where the lovers all are",
A dream of the Adriatic
Wrecked by the discovery of oil –
Discarded oil pumps, slimy canals
Littered with garbage, rusting bridges,
But the tideline glittering like tinfoil,
Men swinging from trapezes, jogging,
Winos asleep against columns.

A skeletal dreamland,
Arcades and palaces slithering
From one vision to another, a pier
Gone up in smoke. Your face
Softens with sun, loses its defensiveness.
Over cupolas and domes
Fashioned out of air,
A harness of green light.

In Windward Avenue, on verandahs
Of wood houses, cats bask,
Wearied by marauding. Sunday
Is a theft of oblivion, boardwalks
Papered with sports pages,
Runners at Santa Anita, saltmarks.

We have come a long way
To go back into the memory
Of each other, among derelicts
And junkies, health freaks,
An afternoon foundering in bronze.

Without the dream, nothing
Is worth it. This vinous
And dilapidated suburb, a shanty-town
Licked by the Pacific,
Lives off a past never completed.

Let us finish what we started.

Stopping in late afternoon to break
The long drive to Tijuana, we entered
At San Juan Capistrano one of those
Dark bars lit by lamps in the shape of
Galleons with parchment sails. At the counter
A group of women habitual
To this coast, once "something in films",
Their prettiness drained by the drink
And the hustling, but in amber glow
Swimming to the surface. Voices grown slurred
And nasal they droned about prices,
Talking over men at their sides
As if they were invisible. "Harry's been
Not too well lately, he misses the business,
Don't you Harry?" and Harry, silent the while,
Turns on his mechanical smile.

JOHANNESBURG, CALIFORNIA

East of Bakersfield, a veldt-like scrub
Scattered with Transvaal names. Tin shacks
Off wide streets leading to nowhere,
A crust of grey dumps, and rickety buildings
Like old film sets pushed into service
In despite of a plot.

Somewhere the imagination,
Like the gold, ran out here,
Ghost town of the Twenties –
Chevvies and hard hats,
Blacks and whites drinking together
In saloons, sharing a piss.

What remains is
A colourless African light,
Disused mine shafts,
A handful of people, like hens,
Scratching out a living.

Faint echoes of whores' laughter,
Sadness like a signature.

Waking early to light filtering
Mineral-water blue, palm trees like bent tin
In a toy oasis, we become aware
Of bluebottle buzz of traffic down Tahquitz-McCallum,
California Angels on their way out to Sunrise,
The sound of horses clop-clopping
From stables on Toledo, following old water-trails
Along Coachella Valley, out to Indio.

All night I had dreamed the Mojave,
As if still driving, eyes hypnotised
By the black strip of tarmac
Stretching like liquorice through gullies
Of the San Bernardino, stones glinting.
Nothing could have been less propitious
Than the outlying approaches
To this sea-level city, grey outcrops
Brought to abrupt halt by cliffs
Sheer off the desert, the sun shuttered.
Wind flapped like a sheet, salt-laden, dusty.

But at dusk the whole plain,
Tilted like the deck of a liner
With lights blazing, filled up with shadow,
Loose outlines of date palms
Inked against the mauve overflow
Of sunset, turquoise orange neon
Flashing from gas-stations, bars, motels,

Car headlamps swinging like beams
From lighthouses. And strangely,
In this oily, extravagant spill,
You sense what had brought the Indians,
The inkling of water, their presence still.

San Jacinto saddle-shaped above them,
Their villas climb out of the plain
On each other's backs. They settle
Among boulders like huge puff-balls,
The rubble from quarries. Cabbage –
Palms spike the cool air.

What they hope is that
They are the last under the stars,
The road running out
Where they've wedged their adobe-styled
Shacks – burglar-proof,
Wired-off, like military outposts.

Their long cars edge
Out of China Canyon awkwardly
As tanks. Under sky
Close as a roof, huge birds
Wheel on predatory patrols, the tongues
Of guard dogs the same
Bare pink as the sparse roses.

CENTRAL HEATING, MANHATTAN

The boat that one will never take,
Beyond the breakers, motors idling . . .
In the early hours I wake,
As so often before, to the creak
And thump of the heating, the thin
Mosquito whine of the elevator.
And always that same image,
The sound of surf, slips
Under my eyes, the beach,
The boat, just out of reach.
Doors click, like cells shutting
On an escape route long
Contemplated, already closing.
Yet I know it's simply the heating
That pushes me to the idea
Of boats' engines, the bay,
The crew one keeps waiting.

The getaway has been postponed
So often one ceases to believe in it.
The self is the same self
One cannot escape from, but drags
Like a salesman from door
To door – an outmoded item
No one has any use for.
I lie out the night, Manhattan
Advancing out of the dark
Like a liner, glassed-in
And spectral, as if covered
In icing. The walls of my room
Are a sickly green, wet
To the touch. The T.V. screen

Has a blank predatoriness,
Hatching out presences.

At five a.m. everything is alien,
Bilge-water and refuse.
There is no warning
System for the imminent collapse,
The silence that will mean
A cessation of heart-beats.
There is no such thing as silence.
We are accompanied into dawn
By inanimate objects intent
On making themselves known,
Radiators, air-conditioners, fridge.
It is the generators that keep
Faith, that ensure morning.

NIGHT SHIFT ON BROADWAY

Emerging after midnight from sour
Stink of subways the shifts
Have changed; earlier,
Threading Times Square from 45th Street,
We moved among crowds
Beginning their night out, neon
Running through them like currents.

Now, stationary in doorways,
The new shift settles in,
Black whores in long thigh-boots,
Blind matchsellers, paper vendors,
Mad women with smokers' coughs,
Couples glued against dime-store entrances.

And those others who simply
Stare straight ahead, at nothing
In particular, sentries
Of the early hours, while around them
Lights flick off in tall buildings.

Indifferent to the recording
Of time and temperature,
Familiars of each other,
These are come to their own
At last – bred in darkness
For darkness, the taste of daylight
Too strong. They return home blindfold.

They stop at intersections,
As if monitoring through earmuffs
Their real news, that comes,
Like their features, from a long way off.
The wind from the East River
Claws at us, smelling of the Baltic,
First Avenue seems a sliver
Of Europe, detached from its moorings.
Down it, shapeless as bears,
They trundle their history.

WALL STREET

Like frogs with relaxed throats
They squat out the day
At the bar in a kind of commode
Position, swapping jokes, reactionary.
They are men on the run,
Fuelled by bourbon and the fear
Of things slipping away from them.
It is hard to imagine the channelling
Of such aggression into tenderness,
The loyalty displayed to their own –
But on afternoons lit
By the glitter and disposal of money,
They show often a flawed
Honesty, a sense of defiance
At what the hunt has done to them.

The wind across Lake Michigan strops
Early morning faces of workers set
As if in cement. You smell
Old wounds, old feuds, the rapacious
And the radical, slaughter of cattle,
Gang warfare. Kicking my heels here
For the late afternoon Super Chief,
Sante Fe embossed on its chocolate-coloured carriages,
I feel the high-wire nervousness
Of this isolationist, anti-British city,
Its ruthlessness and daring – Whitman's
"Ages, precedents have long been accumulating
Undirected materials/ America brings
Builders, and brings its own styles . . ."
Above me, swaying like mastheads,
Glass cones, glass towers, aerial honeycombs.
In Van der Rohe's smoked windows clouds
Sail and dip like schooners, ice-breakers.

But reaching the suburbs is suddenly
To come upon Europe, Lodz, Brno,
Belgrade, smells of sauerkraut
And lentils, news-stalls with *Stern*
And *La Stampa*, onion domes, spires.
The sour odours of exile
Become part of a climate, hanging
Over shopfronts, clothes, like wisps of anaesthetic.

Later, walking the Loop, trains roller-coasting,
I cross Jackson, La Salle – buildings like icebergs
Drifting along Outer Drive, the foam
Breaking up on their sharp edges.

Glass in these aqueous boulevards
Is underwater black, sea-bed green.
Gulls slice past apartment blocks,
The lake whipping itself up under skies
Fired by furnaces of Gary, of Hammond.
In Michigan Avenue shoppers, shapeless in furs,
Waddle on unspecified outings.

And waiting here, between trains,
A handful of hours to dispose of,
Is to have the illusion of seeing
From a great distance, the steelyards
And prairies, lighted windows
With the amber glow animals
Have in their eyes when dying. Feeling the ticket
In your pocket, in your own mind
You have already left, are beyond even good-byes.

In smoking twilight
White patches of cattle grouped
Like cricketers. An end of season
Fullness, the green gathering.

The names on signposts are English,
Romney, Cumberland, Winchester.
But driving towards Washington
Across old battlefields, the ghosts
Are of civil-war soldiers, straggling
Along riverbanks. Incongruously

I think of the Marne,
Hear "bugles calling for them
From sad shires". The greenness
Haunts, in downpour
Turns slowly to mud.

At this hazy martini hour,
Women with pliant eyes
Unwrapping themselves from furs,
Drift of smoke and lazy piano music,
It seems easier to stay –

But soon, lights of New York
Thickening beneath us,
Are flying west, last salmon slits
Of day dyeing the Sasquehannah,
Toledo uncurling like a glow worm,
Omaha spilled seedpearls before nothing.

Lights dowsed now, the cabin
Is scissored by silk legs of stewardesses,
Expressionless robots ministering
With brisk efficiency of night nurses –
They suggest lifestyles
Never quite lived,
Broken promises, failures of imagination.

Half America between us,
I put away what I've been reading
"This is for your sadly missing heart,
The girl you left in Juarez,
The blank political days . . ."
Preparing now for the slow,
Spiralling descent over Nebraska,
Loop of the South Platte river.

Snow clouds, like barrage balloons
Adrift from moorings, move

In on us, our wing tips slice
And quiver, and miraculously soon
Lights of Steamboat and Grand Junction,
Small flares cooled by the Rockies,
Establish our parameters.

With a fly's delicacy
We touch down at Stapleton. Without you
I am completely anonymous,
Companion of a half-empty notebook,
Some paperbacks and clothes. Often
The names of places
Are more vivid than the real thing.

Inhabiting names is a long
Process. We grow into
And out of them. Among the unloading
Of skis it is as a stranger
That I see streams and spruces,
Welcome the cut of iced air.

AT CHEYENNE

On this high ledge of the Laramie
Wind has blown snow into drifts
As expansively white as the breasts
Of a woman slipping her furs
To confront mirrors. The valleys
Are collared by cloud, loose moonlight

Skidding off rock. Looking down
From the snowline the railroad
We travelled hangs like a ladder.
The cold strikes as if somewhere
Broken glass were cutting veins open.

I have thought of you all day
Flying towards me, your head
Full of God knows what –

On the motel bed, on sheets
Stained by other men's semen,
I resurrect half-torn murders
From old newspapers. Obsolete lives,
Like outdated items of sport.

The walls are smeared by insects,
The carpet moults. In the lobby
Women in curlers pad about smoking.

On the closet floor a rolled-up stocking,
Some open-crotch panties. A cabdriver
Spits blood in the courtyard.

Driving downtown I watch
Peachblossom falling like snow –
Soon rain turns to sleet,
To real snow, our wheels dirtying it
Like scorchmarks on linen.

Surprised by the hostility, the anti-war slogans,
The chanting, they loiter on the tarmac,
Dropped from one bad dream into another.

They seem unclear of their part in it,
Cropped heads giving them the air
Of collaborators or criminals. It was not,

Surely, for this they flew into exile,
Became victims or murderers. On this cold
Apron of an airport they exude failure,

Stumble with the distracted gait
Of somnambulists, imagining perhaps
Green jungles they were more at home in,
Ghost cities they may even have loved.

Port of sea-salve on stone graves, oil caves,
Tides on their last murmur of stone slate.

So much for names, Galveston, and those longings
"For islands where must lead inevitably
Blue latitudes and levels of your eyes",
Mexico to the south floating gold syllables
Of treachery turned into temples.
It was as if we had come by chance
On this dank outpost, Dante's *"loco d'agni luce muto"*
Seapinks and sagebrush suffused by sulphur,
Smokestacks of Port Arthur fuming the horizon.

And "the Gulf" – *accidie* of somewhere
Run out of energy, a sense
Of things rotting, boats upended in marshes,
Warped jetties. Yet once a city
For the discerning, in colonial finery,
Mansions in tall trees domed like mosques,
Castles of baronial gothic, chateaux, pagodas,
Boarded up now against ravage and looters.
Among flaking columns and cupolas dogs bark
In overgrown shrubberies, wild heirs
To a magnificence oil put an end to.

SAN ANTONIO

A garrison revived by water,
Walls looped by the Paso del Rio,
Canals with sewn stars as in flags
Of the Confederacy. Here, daily,
As attraction for tourists,
History becomes ritual, coloured slides
Of the Alamo, Santa Ana routed
In the siege of San Jacinto –
A culture mythologised by sacrifice,
The Last Stand – Davy Crockett,
Jim Bowie, rattle of gunfire repeated.

A border post, within earshot
Of Mexico, Spanish
In the walk of its women,
Barracks spattered with bullet-holes,
Ruined Missions. And through dripping palm trees,
Plazas heavy in magnolia,
Vanilla-scent of girls, faint carry of bugles.

You woke with a high fever,
Your ribs in my arms
Like the ribs of foals. Dreading departure
You screened confused images
From our journeys, sternwheelers
In the Ohio river, landscapes
Of Lincoln's childhood, Jefferson's Farmington,
Whinnying of stallions after tornado,
Their manes become clouds, the churned
Wakes of paddlesteamers. Trees
Crashed in your head, hooves pounded,
And everyone was running for cover,
Refugees like us, running into Indiana.

For him, who is above preliminaries,
It is no more than the seigneurial
Raising of hooves round a mane,
A brief thrusting. He strolls off,
Lordly as the sun, indifferent now
To the mare, her bride's eyes dying.
But for that other, amiable,
Grey around the lip, who never
Quite made it, civilities
Of courtship are what he must settle for –
Eyes hazy with love-light, the nuzzle
Of arched necks, legs quivering
As if caressed by cool breezes. She bridles,
Looses her urine. And removed from her,
Pawing stubble in the distance,
He must comfort himself with a suitor's
Dwindling euphoria, remembering
Her shiver, sweat drying on his skin.

OLD FRANKFURT PIKE

In paddocks off the old Frankfurt Pike
We watched mares galloping with their foals,
As if attached still. The foals stopped
When they did, mirror-images dwarfed
By the heat. Encased in light
They looked weightless, eyes floating
In transparencies of smoke, loose blue
At the pupil. Flanks glistened.

And stopping to admire
Their harnessed fluency, mares cruising
In the shadows, radiantly protective,
Foals leggily exuberant, snatched phrases
Of inherited actions, they seemed
Embodiments of the free life,
Their own music. At dusk they drank cool,
Were led home. Only next morning
Did we learn of the fires
That swept through their stables,
Leaving us their whinnying, whites of rolled eyes.

GARDENS OF SOUTH CAROLINA

Soft cobwebs of Spanish moss
Dependent from cypresses, as if mad flocks
Had stampeded through swamps,
Fleece hooked by the sharp branches.

After winter, the hallucinatory South –
Rattan chairs on verandahs, bead
Curtains, magnolia swelling to surf.

Woods barbered to the bright metal
Neck of the river, lakes in the shape
Of butterflies, those long avenues

Entered as in dreams, whose spectral outhouses
Amplify the shuffle of slaves,
The harsh voices of overseers.

Echoes halt in these empty plantation houses,
Ghosts walking their terraces
Immune to erosions of privilege,

The still blending of seasons.

Flush to the Wilmington these greens,
Deepening under sprinklers, take on
A velvet frostiness, a sheer bloom.
Areas of worship conjured from plainness
In a huge country, pampered
And caressed they lie placid
As lake-water in landscapes quiet as convents.
These are the nature reserves
Of America, the competitive
Harnessed to the orderly, the lion
Lying down with the lamb, the rattler.

In Illinois and Oregon they rehearse
These dream territories, briefed
For the cedarwoods and doglegs,
Lush fairways cleaving through blue sea-frets,
The river interrupted by palm trees,
Chipmunks shinning up oaks,
Green phased out in magnolias.

Through long winters they go through
Imaginary rituals, take warmth
From playgrounds made legendary by Nicklaus
And de Vicenzo, Palmer, Player,
Trevino, on sleepless nights
Study angles with navigators' eyes,
Debate irons and woods, run through repertories.

And I watch the jets circling Savannah
In tropical thunderstorms, decanting them
On their four-day packages, surprised

By the Spring and the steaminess,
But ready to take on anything,

To put a good face on it.
Soon they are out in lumberjackets
And peaked caps, bright sweatshirts,
Sunburn coming up on them like birthmarks,
The wind fresh off the Wilmington.

At dusk, shrimpboats slither for the Sound,
The river become a bolt
Of silver spiked by reeds.

In hotel rooms they shower bodies
Ringed at neck and elbow,
The nude flesh in long mirrors
White as if singletted.
And later, at a teak bar
Tended by black barmen they rarely notice,
Their characteristic roughness
Drops from them like skin, whisky
And exercise working their wonders.
Through cigarsmoke they recall old heroes,
Harry Vardon, Walter Hagen,
Compare Johnny Miller and Tom Weiskopf.

Their women, used to segregation,
Have the bleached air
Of marigolds left too long in the sun.

But next day, some before breakfast,
Eggs sunny side up, waffles and syrup,
They are out on their trolleys,
Sniffing the freshness, lakes incised

As half moons, fairways immaculate –
A ball fades in the blueness,
Hanging as if parachuted, then plops
Like a pheasant dropped by a gun-dog.

In the pro-shop and club room
Rummaging through displays
Of equipment, starched whites,
Spiked shoes, check pants,
They take imaginary swings
With new clubs, over cokes
And coffee linger among accessories.

High noon and lawnmowers like cicadas,
Abundance of blue. Then, punctually,
In late afternoon, the build-up
Of clouds over the Atlantic,
A conspiratorial whisper of bamboos.
Thunder breaks the sky open.

An hour later, slopes
And gullies streaming, the sun
As if nothing had happened
Draws off the water.
But it's over for the day,
And they retire under rainbows
Bright as candy
For the comfort of Bourbon and brandy,
Easy after their endeavours.

In the last dusk of hibiscus
And lilac, the air enamoured of itself,
I watch them stream north
In their jets, back to winter

Or what's left of it,
Something of the South rubbed off
On them, an association of images,
Spring with a shimmer of irons,
The bamboos still after thunder,
The languorous couches of greens.

Waterways haunted by exiles
From Batista's Cuba, boats like old slippers
Off neat lawns, palms hinting
Of desert. And at nightfall
Irrelevant men shuffling canals,
At tables sitting out the
Death of a culture, solitaries.

The creeks are sown with neon.
Faint flap of sails, car horns,
A climate suitable
For ending or beginning, become
The same thing. Sadness
Like a deposit at the bottom of glasses.

Cuba Libres. In America
It is always of elsewhere that one thinks.

Turning for home, at last off the bridle,
They seem as they lengthen their strides

Almost to falter. Beneath them, green thickens,
Goes drowsy, as though a film

Were being slowed, the frame frozen.
They have for a second the air

Of somnambulists, moving loosely
In envelopes of water. An uphill element

Is against them. They break free,
And their actions, recovering, turn languorous,

Muscles slithering in quarters
Transparent under sweat, their veins swollen.

Palmettos and flags become fixed blurs,
And towing in their slipstreams long shadows

They dent distance as it dwindles,
Air, earth conniving, eyes limitless.

FLORIDA STORM

Out of nothing but the faintest
Of bruises over Nassau,
A shiver of breeze, then thunder –

Soon the whole area
Slides with the impact of water,
As if someone after a downpour
Were tilting a tarpaulin.
Palm trees under pummelling of rain
Splay out like half-peeled bananas.

An hour later, back in thin air,
Lawns reclaim greenness,
Pools vanish as if blotted.

Tornado country. A gold coast,
Weather-eye permanently cocked.

In starched white, hair bleached,
She leans by a just-open door
In the men's lavatories. Filing her nails,
Assessing my halting approach she calls
"Hi, come right on in, this is the place",
Continuing her filing as I enter the stalls.

Fiddling with my flies, I meet,
Slightly turning, her incurious gaze
As she hums a song by John Denver.
I aim to the side in the angle
One pours out champagne or beer.
It's then that the groans begin,
Cries of effort and distress, like the damned
In the Inferno of Dante Alighieri.
She stops humming and inclining her head
Says softly, as if talking a plane down,
"Go to town, Mr Haftel, go to town."

But the groans continue, get worse,
And Mr Haftel starts roaring like a bull
In a slaughterhouse, half prayers, half curse.
She looks in the door, still filing,
Still soothing – "It's hanging real neat,
Mr Haftel, you're doing real sweet,
Don't give up now." There's a screech,
A silence so total I wonder

If Mr Haftel has quietly gone.
But not for long. "Fucking cocksucker,"
He bellows, and she sidles obediently in,
"Come here and settle my breech."
I depart as fast as I can,
Order a Bourbon and branch,
Apprehensive at the outcome. Long minutes pass,

And then, puffing a huge Havana,
Overweight and sweating, in Panama
And white suit, baggy round the arse,
Mr Haftel emerges, staring crossly ahead,
Like the President of a railroad
Or of some consortium dealing in arms.
Held by the elbow, leaning far forward,
He looks daggers rather than dead,

As if by sheer force of his charm,
His ruthlessness, he could make somebody pay
For the indignity he cannot dismiss,
Like an employee, but must live with,
The plain woman, wardress and bride,
In starched overalls always on his arm,
Far removed from consorts of his manhood,
The tall secretaries summoned to his side.

"A coaling station" where "the air smelt
Of the Gulf Stream". So Dos Passos, in the 20s,
To Hemingway, house-hunting. But a place,
Still, to recommend, though the ferries
No longer leave for Havana, on the north-easterly
No sickly sweet scent of molasses,
Drifts of tobacco from holds of old freighters.
At dusk, though, we catch its own smell
Of coal dust and hibiscus, watch shrimp boats
Round Spoil Bank for the Dry Tortugas,
On Mallory dock applaud nightly
The Gulf claiming the sun, the green flare-up.

From Boca Chica aircraft at mangrove height
Skim Christmas Tree Island, submarines
Slide out of pens where sponge divers
Once left on their errands. That business
Is over. What remains is a sight
For sore eyes, to ruin yourself gently
Among fishermen cruising for tarpon,
Lushes in louche bars. An end of America,
Red moons swaying over mastheads,
The Gulf smelling of failure, disparities.

Sweeping in a great curve
To the Marquesas, these Keys

Slide off Florida like fishtails.
Bridges bracketing them

Flash with the same silver
As fins slicing past coral.

But the peacefulness, peace
Of blue waters, gentle

Cauliflowering clouds,
Has a predatory air – as if,

Out of sullen swing
And tilt of the swell,

Something might suddenly surface,
Jaws working –

In such lulls do the severing blows come.

Necks ringed with ermine, orange-eyed,
They appear goitrous, business-jowled,
In fact are slender-throated,
Swans in their minds' eye,
Ballerinas cursed with dropsy.

Ruminant on rocks, they blow themselves up
As if to give judgement, seem blackrobed
And impartial, though apoplectic,
About to have strokes. Until,
Impatient with the evidence, at odds
With the idea of their bodies,
Snatch seawards, vindictively selective.

"I play a steady, defensive Zen-like game."

"I'd swim, I'd have my ping-pong,
A French meal if possible, see a Japanese movie."
This picture-album of his *Life*
And Times open on the back seat, it is for him
This March day round interminable hairpins
Above a sated Pacific – Monterey pines
Signalling from precarious cliff-edges –
That we hug the road south,
Carmel to Big Sur to L.A.,
Whiffs of Villa Seurat over churned blue,
"Cunt in the air", Lepska and Eve and Mona,
Hustling and clap. We riffle the pages
And there he is in his Palisades homestead,
Snug as a bug between Hoki-san and Puko,
Head bald as an ostrich egg, Japanese as ever.
And there again with that buttery
Blonde, against whom he deploys topspin
And cut in rallies going on for ever.
An old guy in a leather waistcoat
Doing watercolours in the style of his cronies,
Picasso and Chagall and Marin, banging
A piano or stalking the coast breezes
In check cap and muffler. The *Tropics*
Seem a long way off, the screwing
And the scrounging, the cafés, but mostly
Those cold hours hunched at the typewriter,
The passion for his own and other people's books.

Lying up here in his old age, "moving
From doing to being", it is not the wry sage
Going blind, bearing infirmities of the body,
Whom we observe in his oceanic hide-out,
But the writer "leaning over his own self"
Engaged in the manoeuvres of remembering.
Dear Henry, wrapped in your shawls,
You cleared out so much of our guilt,
Coarse and exploitive and querulous,
But at your most sentimental and boring
Retrieving with a joke, humanising
The fearful. You laid it on the line
For us, so that we knew the wondrous
And the wounding inhabited the same skin,
We got out of it what we put in.
It is right that in your eighties serenity
Enfolds you, hallowing you with sunsets,
The Pacific gentling you on its cool couch,
A tall blonde, nude as a doll,
Forever at your elbow, returning serves to you.

It was not this Carmel
Of boutiques and bars, villas
Behind trim fences, clipped hedges.

He started from, and returned to, nothing.

Writing endlessly "like a hermit-crab"
In Pacific Grove, alone
After two marriages, he painted
And planted to drown
"The memory of a nightmare.
I don't think I will get over that."

A morning indolent under honeysuckle,
Streets tilting to ocean, surfboarders.

Between Point Joe and Point China
The whistle and booming of buoys.
Fog like fur encased him,
He listened to sea-lions.
In this climate he wrote
About American women "their minds
Of whores, vaginas of Presbyterians".

Reading his letters it is the life
Not the art that affects us,
Moved by the loneliness of jealousy.

Yet, in this coastline
Peculiarly his own, one can allow for
The unfastidiousness of prose,
The roughneck's soft centre.

For he was a true advocate
Of the dispossessed and the immigrant,
The lowly sweating out their lives
In canneries and freighters,
On farms, without rights without tenure.

Bitterness made common cause,
Universalised the private.
There was too much,
And not enough, time
For himself and for others.

The scarred, brick-red valleys,
Pines clawing at the rock face,
Sea-lions barking at Point Lobos,
Fishyards at Monterey –

These became him, not this chic suburb
Dolled up and sportive,
Where we lie in March sunshine
Skimming through his Letters.

The suffering only is constant.

Sometimes a painting tells us
All we need to know
About our lives, and others'.
This morning I looked
At Hopper's *Second-Story Sunlight*,
Twin gables against thickening trees,
A scrape of shingle, and the light,
All winter soft as cotton wool,
Harsh on the verandah's blistering white.

Preoccupied, austere,
He sits in his dark suit,
Reading the paper. He is impervious
To weather, while she,
Straddling the rail, half-bare,
Unlooses her breasts that loll
With the same sway of boats in swell.

The ice is in his hair
And eyes, for her
This first sun calls
Like a tawny god. She smells
At the resinous, sticky air,
The beating Atlantic. On this springy,
Caressive Cape Cod day,
They seem to pass in mid-stream.
There will be less and less to say.

Green of Louisiana scraped from under us,
Green of canals and rice, green of fern
And banana-leaf, green stubble
Edging the Mississippi, green of forest
Ringing lakes mauve with hyacinth:
And, gaining height, swept green blur
Of Breton Sound, swinging north
Across Lake Pontchartrain, Whitman opened at
"Blossoms and branches green to coffins
All I bring", steadying en route
To Jackson, Memphis, mirror of swamps
Flamingo-smudged before sudden inking
Of sky squid-black over Baton Rouge,
The Louisiana Chateaubriand dozed over
On summer evenings, sternwheelers paddling
The delta pushing white lip of bow-wave,
Barges laden with timber. After Yucatan,
Buried ruin of Merida, beaches of Cozumel,
"America isolated yet embodying all, what is it
Finally except myself? These States,
What are they except myself?", bucketing north
In storm, rain lashing the windows,
Flashes over wingtips, beholden suddenly
To climate, salvaging what we can
From shared pleasures, sadness of tropics.

Into Tennessee, and already mansions
Of Washington Street, the Old Spanish trail
Up River Road and Harahan, shacks
Of Chandeleur bleached like old photographs,
The grace that is legacy of the Gulf,
Magnolia evenings, silk swish of women

Among plants in peppermint flare
Before parachute drop of soft dark,
A style that persists like river-smell
Drawing you from verandahs under tall
Palms to the confluence of tributaries.
Already in shudder of landing gear
The South shed like a skin, "I have perceived
That to be with those I like is enough,
To stop in company with the rest
At evening is enough", the delta fading
In Kentucky turbulence, "Sing on there
In the swamp", Spring less than a hint,
Louisiana falling apart in wave
Of waterlogged grey, reversed before breaking.

Learning of your suicide,
The customary calm of your ending
In that methodical way,
The remorseless advance of the enemy
You could not stop gaining on you,

I look up
At your paintings of Iowa,
Cedar Rapids, Des Moines, Omaha,
Remembering my own journeys
Through that unpopulated landscape
West of Chicago – unpopulated
Because she wasn't with me – my notes

So similar to those scratched
In the margins of your drawings,
As if it were them
I travelled through,
Not the real thing, that emptiness
Spilling its way to the Pacific.

You observed:
"Red oxide barns with silver pinnacles"
"Pink pigs bursting from black earth like truffles"
"Ochre sticks of corn stubble"
"Space and sun"

And approaching Omaha
"For sale – Night Crawlers"
"The air of expectation; of probing contacts"
"Extraordinary prevalence of mortuaries,
Neon-lit and glittering like cinemas".

What you drew
Were the black barns and white-timbered houses
Reminding you of Essex,
Snow patches and corn stooks,
Silos erect on the countryside like penises,
The starched white
Fences protective of loneliness.

I am in Iowa again,
Landlocked and frozen
In a numbing death of the spirit –
You knew before your own
How many forms death takes.

FRUIT CRATE LABELS EXHIBITION, DE YOUNG
MUSEUM, SAN FRANCISCO

Nothing could be prettier
Than these romantic and innocent labels
Coloured to suggest the Good Life –
Monks in their Missions under snowy sierras,
Indians in head-dress gazing at the sunset,
Exotic birds perched in palm trees,
And always, in sunshine, the workers smiling –

Or more misleading about the real
Lives inhabiting the idealised images,
Immigrants in their isolated camps,
Croppers with the disoriented air
Of men divorced from their context.

Only in these bland watercolours
Pasted on the spoils of their labours
Does that wholesome California,
Imagined from the ends of the earth,
Become what it promised – their own,
Sweet land, its fruits never bitter.

A litter of racquets and shoes,
That rubbery, changing-room smell
Half-sexy, half-sour – faint swell
Of your breasts in the shower,
A vein like a bruise.

A view to catch at the throat,
Lighthouse and palms and boat
Rounding the point, the blue
In a sheet clutching at sea-pink
And tamarisk, the ink
Curve of the horizon.

And I remember, sweat pouring from us,
Gravel raked
By your forehand, the gratuitous
Prolonging of rallies for sake
Of the dialogue, its sweetness
– your feet blistered and shoeless –
Setting up the kill.

The strokes that drew blood
Were not the intended ones, rather those
Never quite true, which surprised us –
The afternoon running to seed,
Sky squid-like and rose
At the edges, your need

Unscrupulous and sudden.
The light and the room fade.
But what we once made there,
Clawing at each other, like some musk
Squeezed from our entrails,
Drifts in the dusk, wave after wave.

I watch you writing postcards
Intent as a child doing homework.
Rain, coming up from the Keys,
Herringbones the glass, a blur
You swim out of, shaking hair
From your eyes like a dog.

Absorbed in your task
You write yourself
Out of my presence – you are where
Your cards go to.

Along Biscayne Bay boats move
Between palm trees splayed at the fork
Pale pink of negro's nails.

And lying on our bed,
Swilling my bourbon,
I sit out your absence,
Suddenly hollowed
By what it might be like.

"You know," my mother once said,
Starting and ending a conversation,
"I never really loved your father."

If only I could convince you,
Now on the edge of everything,
That to want to keep
A relationship just so,
Is not lack of love,
But a fear of its changing.

"You are everything to me"
You said, eyes stricken
At my leaving, when my leaving
Was no leaving at all.

From the bed I reach out
For the softness
At the back of your knee,
The cuirass of high bones,
Roughed by the Atlantic,
Over breasts caught by the sun.

Cards finished, you smile,
Returned to a present
We differently inhabit, but share,
Ignorant of perspective.

The hum of the escalator,
And eight storeys up
I watch you along Biscayne Boulevard
Clutching your postcards. Cadillacs
Cut you in half, pushing
Bow-waves before them, like tugs on canals.

The icebox turns itself off,
And separated from you
My heart, disconnected, stops –
The breakers crash in the Sound.

And it has come to this,
Months, or a lifetime later,
The real you in my arms
Behind the photograph of you writing
With that schoolgirl intensity,

Rain streaming down the glass,
The window a green blur,
And your eyes in reflection
Painted like the eyes on fishing boats
For good luck, to illuminate darkness.

I have need of them now
When your going
Has put my eyes out like lights.

VIII

Situations

The season's over and the ferries on the Wislaw
Have packed up. Their crews, in company
With wives, children, dogs,
Loll on deck, picnicking.

Wine bottles steal the sun,
Wafts of salami, gherkin, fresh bread.

Wawel Castle shivers on still water,
Leaves rust underfoot. In Kasimierz,
The ghetto quarter, ghosts accompany us.
Synagogues and cemeteries

Rehearsal to the sealed-off hissing.
There are no postcards.

Blyskawica, rust running from its name
Like soupstains. Whiffs of pomade
From the galleys, bare backs
Shiny with grease in battened-down mess decks.

Missals on lockers, views of Lodz,
Pin-ups on bulkheads. An interim life,
Like our own, top-heavy.

Scraps of Polish drift from the bridge –
Uwaga; niebezpieczeństwo; tam –
Alterations of course, of speed,
Tall tales. The Baltic
Light years off. Staring through seaglasses
They sift smoke from bombed cities.

Rotations of radar, of asdic.
Imagined coast lights of Szczecin,
Seas breaking under moonlight. There is talk
Of homecoming, leave taking,
Speech a mere muttering of syllables.

GDANSK SHIPYARD

A nudity of gesture, the legendary
Aura of togetherness thinning into autumn.
This skeletal skyline, cranked up
For nothing, shuffles out of cloud,
Drops into water. In Raduna dry dock
Eastern Promise and *Allerton* from Taiwan
Bare their propellors. At this tail end
Of summer, blue running out of steam,
Light settles on rust, ignites leaves.
The heroic inflates, turns bleak.

AMETHYST

Your fingers resting on my wrist
Scarred by the suicidal gesture
The marks of which you kissed,

Trace with fallible veins
In inks of eyes or ocean
Names of stone and ship: *Amethyst*.

Anticipating our zigzag, as if somehow
By information or low

Cunning, she knew our speed
And course, she demonstrated a need

For company. She came at us
From all angles, silently, without fuss,

A whine on the asdic, homing in.
We readied depth charges, prepared

Our "tin fish". She moved away,
Out of the sea's swing and sway,

As if hurt, a rebuffed lover,
Whose hide-and-seek was over.

We never fired, nor she either,
Her hull like wet liquorice slipping

Fathoms below us, her bleeping
A reminder like the weather

Of death's attention. In dreams
Her name haunts me sometimes

"You, too," a familiar that rhymes
With everything, except what it seems.

The ship reflected in their eyes,
Pink-rimmed and bloodshot as they row
To safety, it is not smoke that dries
On their cheeks but tears: a score
Of survivors unable to look back.
Screws rotate in air and, nose first,
Helpless against the Arctic thirst,
She plunges, churned waters suddenly slack.

After so many years
That trail of scent,

Half-cloying, half seducing,
Confined in its torso

Of a bottle,
Its shocking-pink label.

After so many years
Its power to revive

Feelings, convey absences,

As if one was coming
To romance for the first time,

Scent lying on her like a stole,

Bare shoulders in the shape of the bottle,
The then of her inside,

Captive in all its deceit.

*"The prettiest place I ever saw in my life, at home
or abroad"*
Charles Dickens, in a letter to his wife, Kate

The sea curved like a cutlass,
And through spaced pines a glint
Of blue. "Invisible till 2"
He instructed, and, through
Thick and thin, stuck to it,
Undisturbed, back to the view.

Later, visibility restored,
He held court: Carlyle and Tennyson,
Thackeray. "Much good merriment",
Rounders on the beach, swimming,
Never for a moment bored.

Nor just writing. Daily he frolicked
At the foot of the waterfall,
Showered under a contraption rigged
To his own design. The lace
Of the sea fretted round his feet;
And always Copperfield going on apace.

I hear him sometimes pacing
The bridge, a familiar, distracted humming,
Like a bee drone. He halts, turns
As if whistling up a dog, thinks better
Of it. The pacing resumes.

Waves like tin, discarded violins
Play tunes for dead sailors.
Whistling is forbidden. I imagine him,
Hands behind his back, tobacco-stained beard
Culling air like a motor-mower,
And the rowing movements
Of his arms as he shoots his cuffs.

The old bugger, I think, drifting
Back to sleep, the years between
Lost somewhere, as now his steps falter,
The sea closing over him like a hairnet.

Leonard, I see you as by Rodin, head in hand,
Leaning on a rail. The chipped blue ocean
Repeats the colour of your eyes.

Your usual air was that of one
Whose gaze was inward, storing images
Like paper flowers yet to open.

Your art as batsman was ever one that leaned,
Its secret timing. In conversation
Jokes came without flourish, dry as dust.

A classical method, sideways on,
Head still and left arm high. Parchment pale,
You flourished according to event.

Eloquent as sculpture in your driving, you fended down
Bouncers as you might unruly dogs,
Distracted almost. Now, ruminant on high,

I imagine your ethereal presence,
Feet slightly splayed, left forearm incised,
All heaven in wonder at your repertoire.

F.D. AMR BEY

Open Squash Rackets Champion 1933–38
Egyptian Ambassador to the Court of St James

There, in his name, a desert
Lordliness, this expert
Of the backhand volley:
                    his on-court manners
In keeping with his status.

Dropshots were tender as butterflies
Alighting, wrist and racket
Taut as cello strings. Deceptively
                    impassive
He wrong-footed even as he smiled.

Nile, feluccas, sand,
Ingredients of a style
Adaptable as sails to wind
                    or currents,
The masking of a stroke.

He floated his returns
To hang like parachutes,
Lobs dying in corners.
                    An exquisite
Geometry made Mondrians of his game.

Caressive, with the touch
Of cat or pianist, an aloof
Interloper in his sidewall boasts;
                    his rallies
Made dialectics out of dialogue.

Warmed up by this practising
Of scales, these conversational martini-dry
Exchanges, there came a time
          to end them.
A flick like a full-stop finished it.

Arm confined below shoulder level
As if winged, the slight
Lopsided air of a seabird
Caught in an oilslick. "Late" Gower,
As of a painting by Monet, a "serial"
Whose shuffled images delight
Through inconstancy, variety of light.

Giambattista Tiepolo
In his "Continence of Scipio" created
Just such a head and halo.
For this descendant no confines
Of canvas, but increasing worry lines,
Low gravity of a burglar.

Stance, posture, combine
To suggest a feline
Not cerebral intelligence. A hedonist
In his autumn, romance lightly worn,
And now first signs of *tristesse*,
Faint strains of a hunting horn.

HALABJAH

At Halabjah, like sprayers of weedkiller,
The fighter bombers, Sukhoi 22s, pass
And repass. They spray gas,

In thin air make asthmatics
From sweet vapours. Inhaling iced sky,
Clouds as they fall in each eye,

These refugees drop like tin
Soldiers, neatly, and rust-free,
In earthen boxes they are bound in.

UNVEILED WOMAN

Swathed in black, it is as if
You were veiled, only your eyes,
Kohl-encircled, visible.
An illusion; I am confusing you
With those others who waddle
Out of ruins, eyes mined.

The something forbidden
About black suggests secrecies
Divulged one at a time,
Though here, on this metallic estuary,
It is simply convention.

But you – temporary migrant
From valleys where greenness presides,
Your taste for black underwear,
Black scarves, flesh made ethereal
In concealments of contours,
And all is flutter and grace –

You are acting a disguise,
Deceptively unsexual, ardour
Masked by velleities of mood,
Privacy of non-attachment –
As for these wild geese
Liberal and opulent in their hideaways.

Heads averted like schoolgirls against glare,
Muzzles bonnetted, camels are overtaken by tanks

With moustaches of sand. They have been there
Much longer, their supercilious ranks

Impervious to hurry. They can afford
To take time, strung out in friezes

Like Christmas decoration, all knees
And hobble under their biblical load.

They do not entwine heads or slot
Trunks like elephants to maintain communion

But sway, high-heeled, on automatic pilot.
They have the machine's measure, a union

Bred of the desert. They will see them off
In due course, indifference to water,

Their storing of green, enough
To mock weapons, make infantile slaughter.

Laser-eyed, an amalgam of prongs
And canisters, of armaments shaped
Like suppositories, I scissor noisily,
A demented cicada throwing sand
Everywhere. My pouch bulges with soldiers.

Crab-like and ugly, I earn
No approving glances, and now my parts,
Only assemblage in common,
Show uneasiness. In question
Is allegiance, their varieties of origin.

All the same, none of us relish
Uncertainty. The rockets
In my belly itch,
Dust gathers in the sockets
Of my barrels. Their long noses twitch.

Like lengths of spaghetti or croquet hoops,
Pipelines stacked on the jetty.
Around them, cranes in suspension
Claw like dentists' drills.

Containers are less than their shadows
Under sky the colour of putty,
And heat, swooning to mirage,
Nullifies effort.

Only tankers move in the Gulf
Their wakes unzipping silence,
Their crews mute signatories
To a war at half-cock.

BASRA DUCK SHOOT

Petrol and papyrus; their smell
Wraps round our bows,
Flotillas of clouds
Reversed onto water.

Oars creaking, we nose channels
Manufactured by mallard. The light
Has the look of varnish,
A sheen as of nylon.

Snakes rustle in the reeds,
Metallic as shot guns,
And, their lives in our hands,
Ducks turn turtle.

More mongrel than whippet, their raked line
Topheavied by equipment, they slide off

Our TV screens into silver horizons we have
To imagine. Though siblings, they confine

Parental resemblance to displacement, not outline.
Like racehorses, they carry in their frames

Ancestral images, bear the same names –
Cities, counties, hunts – reinstated

Generation after generation, liquid green
Memories drawn like a wake, undated.

It is impossible not to fear for them,
Names we once shared, similarly slicing

An ocean, heat not of our essence,
But cold, and the sea-floor's icing.

Huge ironing-boards with stuck-on insects
      Ready on order to peel off,
          They suggest
      Waterborne coffins searching graveyards.
Oceans part like surplices, silver reflects

Off strut, fuselage, wing, aerial.
      Overlooked, or from afar
          Through binoculars,
      Planes seem balsa and glue heat
Might melt as they trundle towards hangars,
      Crews crouched in attitudes of burial.

Raked bows that slit rainbow-oiled wakes
      From tankers ahead of them, flare
          Of their foc'sles
      Delivers into shade as though awnings
          Busy accomplices – oilers,
Pinnaces, grateful of respite from glare.

About their lawful or invidious purposes
      At one with flying fish and dolphin
          They scatter aircraft
      At sunset, the sky white with confetti,
Gulls settling on their ballroom of raft.

That winter,
Following the pipelines, we flew south
From Nineveh. Oilwells, domes,
        Flashes of silver
Betokening wealth, prayer, were all
That gave clues to the usurped
Nature of the desert, a handful
        Of oases, ringworms
Of green. At intervals camels
Plodded below us, footprints
Like sponges. Then, twin rivers,
        Tigris, Euphrates,
The colour of thermometers. Flying over it
The Gulf had a kind of innocence,
Its marshes euphoric with birds.

Peering through bougainvillea that sits
On their heads like mob caps,
Monkeys set up advance posts.

Soon, hands to ears, as if telephoning,
They establish links,
At pre-arranged signals swarming

In formation. Temples' bronze domes
Attract them. They pick up stones
With their tails

Hurling them like cricketers,
Wizened business men
On a company spree.

They take over the place,
Noisy occupiers. Quickly bored,
Soon make themselves scarce.

Lear's "rainbow edging" – bodies,
Temples, umbrellas, saris,
Reflections of lungis fluted by water –
Makes of these ghats
Salons, places of ablution.

Dying here takes on an air
Of performance, of celebration
And mourning. In the presence
Of saddhus, among ashes
And greasepaint, gravity grows manic.

That dawn, oars dipped
Softly as eyelashes, we slid ghostlike
Through mist. Buffaloes surfaced,
And carcasses, the river,
Processional in its wateriness,

Lolling with heat. From life
To death just a pull
Of the oars: past bodies shuffled
And burnished like bugles, a glide
From anointment to obituary.

BIROHI

"Birohi": the lover separated
From the beloved, a concept
Dear to Hindus. An ideal state,
Even, attachment watered
By memory, ideas of renewal.

Yet the present has demands.
Here on the Hooghly, as elsewhere,
Where bodies reacquire innocence,
The past rid of imperfections.

"Birohi": in Bengal
Elevating the inevitable. And but
For such flash floods
Of sudden green spilled
From your eyes, I might concur

In the advantages, the comforts
Of postponement. But "Birohi"
Is abstraction and neither memory
Nor future is match
For the here of your entwining,
Heartbeats held in my hand.

The rose the *mali* fixed in my buttonhole –
The great-grandson of our old *mali*
Who, squatting on his haunches,
Dhoti tucked in, named plants for me –

Was that over-florid shade,
Crimson veined by faintest of inkmarks,
I associate with shaving – my father's cheek
As the razor scraped off the lather.

From cardroom walls
Names of the Fallen drip
In gold leaf, Gurkhas and Pathans.

In the bar, among hunting prints
And portraits of ex-Masters, the demeanour
Of bearers suggests compliance

With ritual, absence of the self.
The Past is itself absent,
Except for its aura. Outside,

On the verandah, among rattan chairs
And stuffed tigers, the Suggestion Book
Gathers dust at the entry,

Ignored, of Rajendra Singh,
Colonel, "Could not potatoes be kept hot,
Should we wish second helping?"

The *maidan* swills green under dust,
Swarming at their throats.
Masts of Hooghly boats
Ghost into dawn. All night

Along Chowringhee the hoarse cries
Rasp at the darkness. Beneath arc-lights
They stagger under great stones,
Moon coating their bones,

The palmettos of ribs. What they're tunnelling
To conclusion, nakedness picked clean
In sweat's marmoreal sheen,
Is what passes for their lives.

WHITE PEACHES

There was the Rhône, neat barges
With gardens imitating real life,

A collie so brushed its coat
Flowed like water.

At a fruitstall we fingered
White peaches, their unbruised flesh

Headier than man-made scent.
Today, months later, I picked one up

Again, hesitantly, and it was as if
All this time the scent of you

Had been stored in the soft skin,
Its aroma bottled and dated.

IX

Departures and Discoveries

RABBIT BREEDING IN TALLINN

"After servicing the doe,
The buck falls off
With a coughing noise."

The handbook is explanatory.
Now, in the next room
Of this Soviet-style hotel,

There are coughing noises,
Grunts of satisfaction.
At breakfast two stout ladies

Descend for their *schinken*.
Something is radically wrong
With politics and the plumbing.

They come in from the country
To hawk furs and blouses,
Roses in cellophane.

Bulky as prop forwards,
Countenances razored by wind,
They stand still as sentries

Under bullet-pitted walls,
Demure as debutantes
Waiting to curtsey,

They bring whiffs of the farmyard,
Prostrating themselves on the floors
Of churches, doughty believers.

The roses we buy
Bring colour to the cheeks
Of our sour-smelling room.

TCHAIKOVSKY'S BENCH

Pyotr Ilyich Tchaikovsky died of cholera,
25 October 1893. On Africa Beach, Haapsalu,
a bench marks the place from which the
composer, on summer visits, used to watch
the sunset.

A kind of lagoon, airless in summer,
Swans desultorily paddling. A sea-green,
   peeling casino,
Gnats flecking salmon-pink sky.

Facing west, inscribed with his likeness,
A few bars of the 6th Symphony,
His bench weathers under pine.

On his last visit, the century
And the season nearing its end,
There was no inkling –

Operas under way, romances
And pick-ups in sweet harness,
Footmen and farm boys.

Water as always conducive
To composing, ideas in spate.
"I have a predilection," he wrote,

"For songs of wistful sadness."
Insidiousness of water, "nil by mouth",
Silver of birches, light ebbing.

At Haapsalu, the end of the line.
A red carpet for the Tsar
Summering here in 1909.

The platform wanders into undergrowth,
A saloon extended for their Highnesses,
Assorted dignitaries.

Saracenic in its filigree,
The booking hall echoes
To the hammering of carpenters.

The old track is grassed over,
Peed on by itinerant dogs.
An idiot punctually turns up

For a train that never arrives.
The end of the line,
Of a summer without hootings,

Without pageantry, a gradual
Denuding of ornament, of icons
And incense. A scatter of the faithful,

Old railway employees, filling in time,
Do duty for passengers,
Absent, mourning the sublime.

One of those mornings
The sea cleaned flat
As if with a palette knife.

On the horizon carbon smudges,
Slight swell like an exercise book
Scribbled on by ships.

On board, her officers imagine
A coastline invisible to foreigners,
A discoloration of sea

Suggestive of land.
On the breeze they hear
Rustle of birches, running water.

SNOW

Entwined like seahorses
We dream the history
Of the fjord; saboteurs,
Ski-troops, limpet-mines,
Bears making a show
Of solidarity, quislings.

Snow makes us light-headed,
Snipers with eyes of monkfish
Cuddle confiscated breviaries.
Eyelids protect us from sun,
Your body a sanctuary.
Outside, real snow has begun.

So faint the scent
She gave off, it seemed breathed
From the lining of her jacket,

Musk emptied of itself,
Mere irritation of air.

Gold epaulettes, ankle-length coat
That swung like a dancer's,
Fur hat with ear-flaps,

In the wreckage of our foc'sle
She was a spectral presence,
Stokers open-mouthed

As though seeing things.
Swatch of blonde hair
Brushing her collar,

A voice like iced smoke,
It was as if we had drowned,
Suddenly come up for air.

BERGEN

A city of statues covered
In birdshit, a leprosy
Of snow. Gangrene setting in.

A switchback
Of a port, easier on legs
Of uneven length.

In Torgalmenningen
A clutter of memorials –
Resistance leaders, soldiers
In helmets like tortoises,
Sea-booted sailors.

A fishy music
In the air, infectious.

Streets show black
As keyboards, a thaw
On the way.

Incised by the prows
Of ships, the inlet
Turns skate-rink,
Clanks like cutlery.

The fjord exhales,
Breathing smoke.

There is a taste
On the tongue
Like wafers, a half-listening.

Operation Chariot
for Charles Sprawson

SHOULD THE *TIRPITZ*, at last operational, break out into the Atlantic, only the great Normandie lock at St Nazaire was large enough to receive her. "Operation Chariot", an assault by sea, was devised to destroy it. On 26 March 1942, an ageing, expendable, Lend-Lease destroyer, the *Campbelltown*, with an escort of the destroyers *Atherstone* and *Tyndale*, and in company with an assortment of motor-torpedo boats, motor launches, and one motor gun boat, sailed from Falmouth. The intention was that *Campbelltown*, loaded with explosives, should penetrate the German defences on the Loire estuary and ram the lock gates, blowing them and herself up.

> A mild afternoon, spring nervous
> Among palm trees, advancing
> And retreating. Unremarkable weather,
> Skies clearer than welcome. A huddle
> Of ships that might be trawlers,
> Fishing boats. Looming over them
> *Campbelltown*, two funnels removed
> And slanted in the German fashion,
> Uneasy in disguise. Lightened aft
> To skim over sandbanks, but tricky
> To handle. A dowager in finery.

> Falmouth had been a last
> Run ashore, scones, ale,

Cornish pasties. Back on board
Her bemused crew watched
Finishing touches put to camouflage,
Flags stored with swastika and emblems.

On board *Campbelltown* commandos,
Faces blackened, suffered in slight swell,
The Atlantic building up
On the beam, washing the Scillies.
By nightfall, steering due south
On their 400-mile passage,
They were free of all traffic,
Scurrying cloud mapping the moon,
Silvering bow-waves.

Throb and shudder of engines,
Adjustments to speed, to course.
"Steer 170°." "Up 10 revolutions."
"Midships." Ghostly repetition
Of orders, muffled acknowledgment.

Off Ushant, swastikas exchanged
For the white ensign. Looming to starboard
A scatter of trawlers.
Accordion music and garlic
Drifting from fishing boats.

At first light, the sighting
Of a U-boat, depth-charged
By *Atherstone*. Like a whale
She rolls over, dives deeper.

Hours later, the sea empty,
She surfaces, transmits presence

Of enemy forces. *Campbelltown,*
As a diversionary measure,
Feints to move westward.

Five Möwe-class torpedo-boats,
Alerted, streak from their lair
In St Nazaire, a time-wasting sweep
Past Belle Ile, wrong-footed.

Clouds mercifully thickening,
Cocoa and rum for the run-in,
And that first sense of land,
A lightening of water.
Scent on the wind.

A compromise of ocean.
"Port 10" and then,
Swinging sharply north-east,
A row of lights ahead,
Like a stopped train. Destroyers
Peel off, vanish into darkness.

The tide running high,
So entering the estuary
Was like gliding
Over a sprung ballroom.
MLs, MTBs swoosh
And cavort in *Campbelltown*'s wake,

On possibly their last night
On earth, 62 naval officers,
291 ratings, 268 soldiers,
Muffled in silence,
Hold their breath.

Time at a standstill.
Bow-waves like lip-salve,
All that is visible
As they edge closer,
Screws slithering.

Two miles to go, and now searchlights,
Fingering the darkness,
Pick out each vessel
As if in a circus tent,
Campbelltown, MTBs, MLs.

Morse and Aldis lamps
Stutter out challenges,
And in *Campbelltown*
Leading Signalman Pike,
Specially assigned-German speaker,
Returns challenges in German.
False identification signals, call-signs, implying,
"Friendly forces returning from patrol,"
Stutter from the mast head.

Precious minutes are saved,
The signals interpreted.
Then, suddenly, the whole sky
Splattered with tracer,
Peppermint-green, rosebud-pink,
Like a cabaret. No need now
For dissembling, on *Campbelltown*
Instructions ringing from the bridge,
"Full Speed Ahead, Both Engines."

And now, Mindin Bank to starboard,
They skirt the deepest channel,

Come in range of heavy artillery.
Shore batteries, uncertain still
Of identity, hold their fire,
And *Campbelltown*, making 19 knots,
Attendants in place, skims Grande Rade.

Now, if ever, for blessing.
The navigator on ML310,
Chosen for knowledge of the estuary,
Boozy old peacetime yachtsman,
Remembers *La Frégate* and *Havana*,
Hospitable estaminets, their girls
In black stockings and suspenders,
Little else, one with hole
At the heel, bared like an apple.

Remembers, too, a forsaken 14-footer,
The swirl of water between sandbanks,
A blonde arm sharing the tiller.
He knows the way in,
And *Campbelltown*, following,
Surges at the lock gates,
Lit up as if for surgery.

Abreast, a guard ship,
Buddha-like at the entrance,
Now silenced by pom-poms.
Confused, panicking shore batteries
Rake her, crew diving
Into black water. Scuttled,
She sizzles, subsides.

On *Campbelltown* they hoist
The white ensign, swastikas

Consigned to the gannets.
Now gunfire on all sides,
A party grown raucous,
Campbelltown responding with 4.7s,
Oerlikons, Lewis guns.
Commandos, readying for exit, crouch
Frog-like behind gun turrets,
The quay sliding towards them.

At 01.34, on March 28,
Four minutes adrift on the ETA,
Campbelltown, her crew steadying
    themselves
For impact, cut through torpedo nets,
Rammed the lock caisson. Stuck.

For most, a one-way journey,
Though – what seemed a lifetime ago
Among Falmouth's palm trees
And friendly headlands – plans
Had been laid for withdrawal.
Plans only, not cynically made,
Just provisional, reliant on God's grace.

MLs, cutting across shot silk
Of Penhouet Basin, the bows
Of *Campbelltown* embedded,
Land soldiers under stage lighting,
Crews reduced to ants.
Gunboats, like clockwork toys
Gone demented, circle in patches
Of burned oil, the Old Mole
Like a basin blood-filled
After an attempted suicide.

On shore, buildings go off
Like fireworks, demolition parties
From *Campbelltown* laying waste,
Startled sentries up-ended
By rugby tackles. Men stagger
Along quays like drunks
Or headless chickens, bleeding.

The commandos, cut off,
Nowhere to go, roamed
Into captivity or oblivion.
They never had a price,
Token counters in a board game
Invented by others.

Campbelltown, meanwhile, nursed
    wounds,
Bombs foetal in her hold,
Crew captured or hiding. Like a dog
Wanting to be put down
She lay on her side, mute.

Next day, at noon,
Decks thick with German officers
Inspecting their booty,
Imagining the exercise over,
She blew up, taking them with her.

An expendable ship, chosen
For her expendability, but reliable,
With her last breath wiping
The smile off the face
Of her visitors, a delayed welcome
Removing the cream of them.

She went down unattended,
Alone, what remained
Of her crew too distracted
For the tears that she merited.
Around her lay fragments
Of gunboats, bodies floating
On wreaths of refuse.

Sailors have no recycling,
Calculated sacrifices
For whom trumpets may sound
Across oceans, but whose
Simple ambitions, pleasures
In drink and swearing,
Sink with them. Not for them
The luxury of post-mortem.

As a result of the attack on St Nazaire the Normandie dock was rendered useless for the rest of the war. U-boat headquarters and all German naval operational centres were shifted inland in fear of an Allied landing.

In Operation Chariot the Royal Navy lost 85 men, the army 59, out of a total force of 630. The 106 sailors and soldiers taken prisoner included Lieutenant-Commander S. H. Beattie, captain of *Campbelltown*, who received the VC. German losses, as a result of the explosion in *Campbelltown*, and the repeated torpedoing of the lock gates by MTB74, were reckoned to be higher.

Today the neglected naval port of St Nazaire, on either side of the flat banks of the Loire estuary, bears no record of these events. They are old history. The cafés and restaurants remain, but there are few sailors. My own interest derives from the same year as Operation Chariot, since my first ship, the V. and W. class destroyer *Vivien*, was commanded, before his posting to *Campbelltown*, by Lieutenant-Commander Beattie.

SMOKING

Gazing riverwards he flicks a cigar butt
On to the mud, a faint brssz as it hits.

He takes in a screen of trees, the struts
And filigree of bridges, a moored barge.

A water tower, the Scots baronial Lister Hospital,
T. S. Eliot's old lodgings, shiver on his eyes.

Part of a reverie, this Chelsea seascape
Where nothing quite registers, or is over.

Absent from himself, the dull impact
Of tobacco on slime alerts him, recalls

Just such an evening off Sheringham,
Leaning over the rail, smoking.

A breeze flounces water into petticoats,
There are figures in the wake, gesticulating.

They have unique brakes, juddering
To a halt with the noise
Of rubbery foghorns. In the early hours,
Sleepless, they cruise Beaufort Street,
Light on the river behind them
Like marbled endpapers, swilling
Under bridges. On such nights
In convoy ships lowed like cattle,

Sixth senses warning of proximity.
Hearing them I wake sweating.
In Battersea the gold Japanese pagoda
Looms out of darkness, mist patches
On plane trees like sheep's wool
Caught up on barbed wire.
Water slips back on itself.
There's a sense of light lifting.

The 45s pass, outward and homeward,
Acknowledging each other with toots
On their horns, like sister ships
With their sirens. Drivers exchange pleasantries,
Stop for fags. On this nocturnal
Cross-river route they are like pilots
Nosing an estuary, at ease with themselves
And each other, co-conspirators.

DOG-LEG

for Polly

Front paw hung limp
As a stage curate's handshake.

That blue evening a blur
And thump of metal, mud like make-up.

Now veteran of the trenches,
Hobble-skirted, she stutters on hind legs.

And where dreams propelled her
In fruitless pursuit, ears streamlined,

Only twitches of muzzle
Convey excitements of the chase.

Lying sideways this evening, pads
The texture of throat pastilles,

Coat still shiny as oilskin,
Black as liquorice,

She shapes herself
To accommodate a chaise-longue.

And what she misses
Only occasionally surfaces

As in eyes of penitents
Pleading for forgiveness.

A CALCUTTA OFFICE

Entering my father's old office
In Bankshall Street, the cries of paan sellers
And Hooghly steamer sirens
Drifting through shuttered windows,
I feel like a thief –

The desks in the same places,
The punkahs revolving, peons on their stations,
But the whole room shrunken,
As if by his absence, an empire meanwhile
And himself come to grief.

Like temple gongs muted by ocean
They begin singly, swelling in unison,
Kling huey, syar huey,
Remorselessly repetitive.

Underbellies like the shifts of Cantonese
Clerics, they put themselves about,
Puffy politicos with palatine teeth.
Goitrous, they blow themselves hoarse.

They are indifferent to distant wars.
But in their nocturnal antagonisms
Tree frogs and cicadas, old rivals,
Provide scale,

Their choruses of squabble
Mere irritants. In these green choirstalls
Light thins from banana leaves,
Conflict reduced to hushed sibilants.

FOREIGN LEGIONARIES AT CALVI

Like filmstars of old, képis tipped
Forward over colourless stubble,
They suggest forts abandoned
Among sand dunes, camel trains, bugles.
Le jour de gloire est arrivé.

Their tattoos bear cliché images,
Girls' names, Marie, Chantal,
As if words might make real.
Dragons and mermaids slide over muscle.
They remind of Claude Rains and Gabin.

In camps off this fabulous bay,
Wired off like chicken runs, they drill,
Oil guns, strip engines.
Waiting for posting, they top up
Suntan, challenge in beach races.

Whatever regrets about joining,
It's always too late, their geography
Initialled by misdemeanours, history's
Accounting. We watch their lorries revving,
Mostar and Sarajevo scrawled on their sides.

CAPE GOOSEBERRIES

A sly, surreptitious taste that dries
In the mouth, dust overtaken
By a sourness turning sweet.
Their leaves are papery, scrotal.

A guest at Simonstown naval base
In the Cape, I first tasted them
The day my old shipmate
Began his sentence. Robben Island
In the distance, Table Mountain under cloud.

I remember only the fruit's acidity,
Their sweetness excised.

Through the porthole I watched
Stout Boer policemen chasing Coloureds
With a stick. They eluded them,
Slithering like eels, then diving
Among bumboats laden with fruit.

Choosing Cape gooseberries now at the store
Off Fulham Road I get a sudden
Sour stink of Africa, sweat
Drying on skins the colour of aubergine.

A sudden regret, too, for somewhere unloved
In the first place but which took hold
With its light, its cruelty, its shabby, flat veldt.

IN OPORTO

On these curved steps pouring
Like watered escalators
To the Douro, girls inject themselves,
Novices under clumsy instruction.
Needles we pick our way through
Litter doorways like spent matches.

Below us banners of wine lodges –
Sandeman, Harvey, Byass –
Turn hillsides into regattas.
On quays awash in rain
Barrels gleam humpily like snails.
Barges wear funerary black sails.

The cloying vinous stink
Around these half-developed children
Masks vomit and blood
In its freefall. Syringes
Catch the last light, wine casks
Bottling a murderous sunset.

BED-SIT, 1946

In postwar days bed-sits
And bedmates changed
With the seasons. Run out of money
For the meter I knocked

On the landlord's door
And entered. He was locked
In the arms of a woman,
Her dress on the floor.

A pink corset encased her,
Thighs mottled by the fire
Which sputtered. Legs splayed,
She was warming her bottom,

Holding a book.
I murmured apology,
She never bothered to look,
An ample, hairy woman

Lavish in the rump.
He was bespectacled and sweating,
Trying to make ends meet,
Reduced to letting.

Among corpses floating downriver
A man brushes his teeth
At a ghat, spattering his dhoti.
Drops on his flesh form like sago.
With rowing motions he brushes off

Paan-coloured petals. From a pitcher
He sluices himself, two fingers
Clamping his nose. A moment of splutter
And gargle, spit made ceremonial.
Pink saris flow behind him

Like ambulatory mummies, their roundness
Of flesh inflating them. They remind
Of Degas, "women drying themselves",
The angles of haunch and elbow,
Water rubbed off skin, purifying itself.

This sliver of riverside, soil soured
By gases, coaldust, sewage,
Home once of sour lives, soiled birds:
In old photos boatmen in cloth caps,
Chokers, loaf down Lots Road,
Faces kippered by smoke.
A waste land of sulphur and whippets.

Less polluted now, evening revives us,
And the river, innocent of traffic,
Salvages something, an elsewhere
Of estuaries, outlets, deliverance.
In subsidence of clamour we become aware
Of community, fraternity of dogs,
The appeasement of bridges.

Light swivels wash of police boats
As if below surface fish struggle
Against netting. Barges loll
In cross-currents, weedy mucus
Of houseboat hulls, of pontoons.
Despite everything, vestiges still of Whistler,
Greaves's dinghies upended in mud,

Oars folded like oiled gannet wings.
And outside the Cross Keys a dipping light
Lends beer mugs a stained-glass glow,
A sepulchral serenity. The tide heaves up
A straggle of boats, a loitering of drinkers
Disperse, and through swing doors
The voice of Donna Summer cuts off.

THE SEA: 1939–45

For Roy Fuller

I

Remembering, the experience in itself seems changed;
    the hundred
broken moments that the mind perceived, grow faint,
absorbed like actions in a dream, severed from fact
into the single fluid movement that the sea contains.
Then, night and day merged like screens above the
    water,
the wind and sky uncoloured in the leadened afternoons
whose hours stretched unemphatically to dusk; the
    surfaces
of wave and cloud, the ships disposed in geometries
of speed held then a sense of purpose and of edge;
but now acquire with time the faded naturalness of hills
or birds flattened on a skyline, contours like memories
accepted in the mind, which now the eye no longer
    notices.
Till, the time and place being changed, the ways of
    living
part, and they appear, images integral to the heart.

II

Then it was, beneath long nights of conflict and despair,
the sea rose softly like a sleep, creating space
and time for thought, a detached, moving stream
through which all personal troubles could be seen
mirrored in water, images no longer hurting, but quiet
as reflections, minute against the power restrained there.
When, helpless under war, the human private world

grew loose and uncontrolled, the mind distorted
with memories of disaster; and, waking, late at night,
the heavy, engined darkness made all life appear
remote, and existence one distinct and separate point in
    fate.
But, absorbed then, the restless brain grew quiet
aware of the sea glittering beneath cold stars
and the horizon lifting gently under the northern moon.

III

Summer, though, found waters moving in blue serenity,
coasts of Norway and Iceland rising stark from the dawn,
the sunrise mists dissolving on a night of phosphorus
and black coral. Convoys travelled here, easily drawing
reflections on the glass surfaces of sea, the silence broken
by the still ringing of bells, the coloured buoys marking
a mine-swept channel. At night, the quiet increased,
only a slight wind ruffling the water intensified
the voices of look-outs, the monosyllables muttered
down voice-pipes. Released, the mind roamed, oblivious
amongst moving patterns of sky and sea, the altering
    formation
of clouds gathering behind stars, the huge ocean.
And, watching darkness grow thin, observed the pale
    straws
of light thickening and the clouds massing on the
    horizon.

IV

Through passages of winter, remembering harbours
    entered

at nightfall, the headlands garlanded with searchlights,
the time seems suddenly condensed and smooth. The
   sharp,
hurried moments of action, the cries of men wounded,
the thundering of guns, remain only as echoes, vibrating
without sound, already unreal and shapeless to the mind.
And we who remain and witness the voyages,
remember the warnings and days of disaster,
and need more than promises and chances of glory.
For the children of children who dream of the ocean
and hear in its singing the songs of their fathers,
the morning must answer with a sea of assurance.
Or else there is no rest for the mocking voices,
and no meaning in the tides of compassion, where
the drowned drift condemned to the fishes.